VLAD DRACULA TAROT

VLAD DRACULA TAROT

TRAVIS McHENRY

ROCKPOOL

A Rockpool book
PO Box 252
Summer Hill NSW 2130
Australia
rockpoolpublishing.com
Follow us! rockpoolpublishing
Tag your images with #rockpoolpublishing

This edition published by Rockpool Publishing, 2021
Originally self-published by Bloodstone Studios, 2020

ISBN: 978-1-925924-97-8

Illustrations by Nikita Vuimin
Edited by Lisa Macken
Designed and typeset by Sara Lindberg, Rockpool Publishing

Printed and bound in China
10 9 8 7 6 5 4 3 2

CONTENTS

INTRODUCTION

When I first began writing this I assumed it would be enough to simply post a short caption next to an image of the tarot card. However, after a trip to Romania and after pushing past the modern historians and researching the original source material, I realised there were stories that had not yet been told, or at least interesting details that had been glossed over by previous Dracula scholars.

In 1992, at the age of 12, I checked out the hardcover edition of *Dracula: A Biography of Vlad the Impaler 1431–1476* by Radu Florescu and Raymond McNally at my school library. I had been completely obsessed with vampires, and Dracula was my favourite. Reading about Vlad's life made him scarier than any bloodsucker in a black cape from the movies, with many depictions striking me as acts of unwarranted brutality. I didn't finish the book.

I bought a copy of *Dracula: Prince of Many Faces*, Florescu and McNally's updated version of Vlad's official biography, and was struck by the way Vlad's life is told in a series of little vignettes due to the structure of the original source material – pamphlets, poems and letters – which present his life as line-by-line expositions of individual atrocities. I thought it would be awesome to create a series of illustrations in the style of traditional woodcuts depicting scenes from Vlad's life that helped readers better understand the true breadth of his rule over Wallachia. I realised many events from his life were eerily similar to scenes from the tarot; for example, the peasant with the ill-fitting clothes seemed like a real-life version of The Fool card, while Sultan Mehmed II and Pope Pius II embodied The Emperor and The Hierophant.

The Visconti-Sforza tarot deck, the art for which has been adapted for all successive tarot decks, was created for the Duke of Milan in 1451, just a few years prior to Vlad ascending the throne as voivode (warlord or local ruler) of Wallachia. Thus the artwork used by the creator of the oldest known tarot deck would have been contemporary with the story of Vlad the Impaler's life and times.

Although this book was intended to be a collection of fascinating pictures and light reading, as I peeled back the layers of Vlad's life I noticed the numerous translation errors that created incorrect pictures of famous events. In the pursuit of accuracy I translated many original documents myself, being confronted by Italian, Old Church Slavonic, German, Russian, French, Latin and Romanian although I don't personally know any of these languages. I passed passages that were in disagreement with established historical record to experts for assistance in confirming or correcting my original translations.

This book is a far more scholarly work than I set out to write. I hope the woodcuts that accompany each story will help set the scene and paint a clearer picture in your mind of who was doing what and when. The world of Vlad the Impaler was a complex maze of political and military alliances that shifted frequently, making friends out of enemies and impaled victims out of former friends.

NOTES

Vlad the Impaler aka Vlad Țepeș aka Vlad III of Wallachia is referred to by the name he himself used and also what he was called by most chroniclers during his lifetime: Vlad Dracula.

The words 'Ottoman' and 'Turkish' are used interchangeably.

Castle Dracula is known as Poenari Castle.

Vlad's father is Vlad Dracul, not Vlad II Dracul.

Romania refers to the entire territory contained in modern-day Romania, otherwise Wallachia, Transylvania and Moldavia are used.

Prince Stephen III held the title 'voivode', but his title is Westernised to 'Prince' to distinguish him from the voivodes of other territories.

Istanbul is called Constantinople except when referring to the modern city, but they are the same place.

Many of the original sources are available online, and the bibliography provides sufficient information for a budding Dracula scholar to begin their quest for knowledge.

O gʒ misericors est deus
Justus et paciens

USING VLAD DRACULA TAROT

The *Vlad Dracula Tarot* can be used like any other tarot deck and with whatever spread/s you feel most comfortable using. Due to the unique nature of this deck there are also special kinds of readings you can do to get the most out of Vlad's life lessons.

PERSONALITY READING

Many of the cards in this deck represent individual people, so if you have a question about a specific person in your life it may be helpful to pick a significator card from among the personalities in the deck that most closely matches the person in your life.

- *Example 1:* Radu the Handsome (Knight of Cups) was a passionate male lover. If you've been dating someone new and want to know how serious it's going to get, Radu would be a good card to base your reading around.

- *Example 2:* Lady Kalinikia (Queen of Stakes) was a motherly figure. If you're having problems with a female family member and want to know the best way to deal with them, this would be a good card to base your reading around.

› *Example 3*: Emperor Sigismund (King of Stakes) was the ruler of a vast territory and commanded the destinies of many princes and kings, including Vlad Dracula. If you have issues with your boss or manager at work this card would be perfect to base your reading around.

READING FOR OVERCOMING WEAKNESSES

Mediaeval Europe was a fierce place to live that required strength and resilience in order to survive. Plague, war and famine were part of daily life for everyone no matter their class or profession.

Choose as your significator a card that is traditionally seen as bad in most tarot decks, such as The Tower, The Devil or the Nine of Swords. As you lay out the cards around it, try to relate to the card from a point of strength rather than acting as a victim.

› *Example 1*, The Tower: we generally picture ourselves as being the person falling from the tower or as though the tower represents all we have built now crashing down. Consider this: Vlad built Poenari Castle over 500 years ago and it is still standing today. Look at the tower from his point of view rather than from the point of view of his wife, who flung herself over the edge unnecessarily.

› *Example 2*, The Devil: how could the rage and downfall indicated on this card possibly be looked at from a different perspective? Quite easily: Vlad the Impaler is the one causing the downfall of his enemies, so instead of viewing the card as an indication of something horrible happening to you look at it as though you are in command of your future.

ORTHODOX CROSS SPREAD

As Vlad Dracula was a member of the Eastern Orthodox Church for most of his life, it makes sense to implement a new kind of cross spread in place of the traditional Celtic cross for this deck.

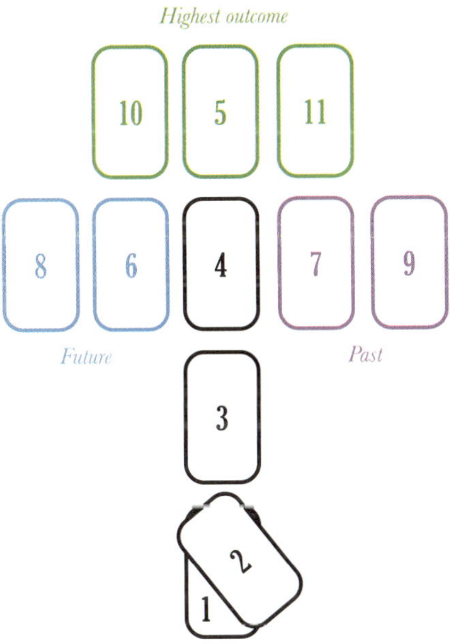

- *Card 1:* the significator forms the base of the cross; everything in the reading will be built upon this foundation.
- *Card 2, crossing the significator:* this card represents the challenges that will have to be overcome in order to achieve the desired outcome.

- *Card 3, above the significator:* this shows the skill or ability that the querent will need in order to achieve the desired outcome.

- *Card 4, above Card 3:* this is the first bar of the cross, forming the basis of future and past events. This specific card represents present circumstances.

- *Card 5, above Card 4:* this is the second bar of the cross; it shows the highest possible outcome and is an indication of what will be.

- *Cards 6 and 7, placed to the left and right of Card 4:* these show the immediate future (Card 6) and the immediate past (Card 7), which will have some influence on the matter in question.

- *Cards 8 and 9, placed to the left and right of Cards 6 and 7:* these show the distant future (Card 8) and distant past (Card 9), which will have some influence on the matter in question although the influence on these events is very weak or has faded away.

- *Cards 10 and 11, placed to the left and right of Card 5:* these complement the top bar and provide increased illumination concerning the future outcome as indicated by Card 5. Together these three cards show a complete picture of the final outcome or answer connected with the question.

MAJOR ARCANA

0. THE FOOL

The peasant and his wife

Vlad Dracula came upon a peasant farmer wearing clothes that were full of holes and didn't fit. Upon hearing from the farmer's wife that he brought home plenty of flax, Vlad Dracula ordered her to be impaled. The peasant farmer pleaded for his wife to be spared, but Vlad said: 'Your wife has been negligent in her duties despite having a husband who works and tills the land. You will be much happier with another wife.' Vlad warned the farmer's new wife to be more diligent in her household duties.

This seems merely another example of Vlad Dracula's cruelty, but it should illustrate the high esteem he placed upon the value of work and labour. He expected everyone to toil for the betterment of themselves and for the collective good of Wallachia.

Divinatory meaning: the meanings of The Fool card, a card of new beginnings, are captured in the story of the peasant and his wife: a fool goes through life wearing ill-fitting clothes but does not care that his garments are making him stand out from everyone else.

Often new beginnings, either positive or negative, come from outside forces greatly disrupting your life. Sometimes the universe knows better than you do that it is time to move forward to a better place, which you can't do unless the previous parts are destroyed or otherwise change.

I. THE MAGICIAN

Vlad Dracula

The 1400s were a time of constant conflict in Europe. As voivode Vlad Dracula had to be cunning, ruthless, diplomatic and financially savvy, simultaneously balancing the needs of his people – the noble class (boyars), the merchant class (Saxons), Catholic and Orthodox clerics and the peasants – against the demands of Wallachia's enemies and allies across Europe and Asia Minor. He created the image of a strong and cruel leader so that internal and external threats could be kept at bay.

Vlad had four tools at his disposal: an army (the sword), taxes and merchant income (the coin), diplomatic connections with Europe and Turkey (the cup) and his ruthlessness (the stake). He employed these elements to maintain Wallachia's independence at a time when it was under constant attack and become a hero to his people.

Divinatory meaning: The Magician is able to change the circumstances to meet his demands by using the four tools of the tarot to alter the world around him and thus become a master of the art of magic.

Taking control of your situation can be challenging and rewarding, requiring you to utilise your skills but also hide some of your abilities. Sometimes what happens behind the scenes will lead to a bigger pay-off, and those talents are better left hidden until after success has been achieved.

II. THE HIGH PRIESTESS

Vlad's Transylvanian princess

Vlad Dracula had two wives and several mistresses. Several historians believe his first wife was an illegitimate daughter of John Hunyadi, a Hungarian nobleman who was Vlad's ally or adversary depending on the current political situation. Vlad most likely married her to help secure his northern frontier against her father, who was partially responsible for Vlad's first exile from Wallachia. She was the mother of his children and was married to him throughout his entire second reign over Wallachia (1456–62), his longest period of prosperity, although there is significant disagreement between historians and the chronicles concerning her identity and the fact of her marriage to Vlad.

The marriage must have served its purpose, because in April 1456 John Hunyadi suddenly shifted gears and supported Vlad Dracula's invasion of Wallachia against Vladislav II, the very man John had installed on the throne a few years prior.

As Wallachia was being invaded by the Ottoman army Vlad's Transylvanian princess took refuge in the well-fortified Poenari Castle. An archer shot a letter through her window that warned that the Ottoman army planned to take the castle by force and all inside should begin a retreat. While Vlad and his soldiers made preparations to sneak out of the castle, his wife threw herself out of the window and died in the river below.

Divinatory meaning: The High Priestess is a strong woman who keeps her power and knowledge hidden. Embodying all the strengths of the female sex, she holds the power of the tarot in the palm of her hand. The queen of esoteric thought and occult practices, she provides revelations to those who come to her throne and has the power of The Magician with the structure and authority of The Hierophant. Self-empowerment through knowledge involves the revelation of mysteries, which is the speciality of The High Priestess. Whenever we receive new information we should properly evaluate it instead of jumping into hasty action.

Not only can The High Priestess reveal mysteries, she is also a keeper and guardian of secrets. This card might indicate a close confidant, one who knows your inner thoughts. If this card is found beside The Hermit or The Moon then there is a potential for future betrayal, and perhaps your relationship should be evaluated.

III. THE EMPRESS

'Let the world see where I have been.'

The gruesome scene depicted on this card concerns one of Vlad's mistresses. She was afraid of losing him to another woman so she told him that she was pregnant with his child. When he later discovered she had been lying about the pregnancy, Vlad ordered her to be cut open, flayed alive and put on display on the public street with the words: 'Let the world see where I have been.'

This act served two purposes: a strong warning not to manipulate the voivode's actions, and a way of verifying that his mistress was not actually pregnant. Vlad's mistress wished to serve as a mother figure but did not actually conceive, and she was punished for her deception. The mistress was made to be literally open and honest after she was cut open by Vlad Dracula.

Divinatory meaning: The Empress is linked to the concept of an earth mother, a goddess responsible for bearing children and procreating; she is traditionally an open and honest woman. In some ways she is the opposite of The High Priestess: soft, caring, nurturing and revealing all she has through the act of childbirth.

Fertility can signify more than just childbirth or family life. It can represent the fertility of career or money, and desire of all kinds: love, sensuality and abundance.

IV. THE EMPEROR

Mehmed the Conqueror

Sultan Mehmed II was a strong, stable ruler in European and Middle Eastern politics who gained the honorific 'the Conqueror' partly because of his successful conquest of Constantinople. Many Balkan monarchs relied on Ottoman support to continue sitting on their thrones; loyalty was considered to be a weakness, and treachery was rampant.

Mehmed became a crucial figure throughout Vlad Dracula's life, serving as both friend and adversary. Although he was never truly defeated in battle against the Wallachian army, he was forced to abandon his master plan to invade Europe thanks to a series of tactical losses at Vlad's hands. However, his diplomatic achievements and military conquests left a legacy that far outlasted his life.

Divinatory meaning: authority and stability and the trappings of royalty and tradition. The Emperor is a strong male figure with absolute power. Most tarot decks depict the Holy Roman emperor as The Emperor, but at this time Mehmed was more dominant.

The Emperor can signify a person in your life who wields some authority over you or someone who will provide assistance; these two may be the same person. An emperor's power is built upon smaller kingdoms that existed before his rule; thus, there may be foundations upon which you have built your current condition that need to be examined.

V. THE HIEROPHANT

Pope Pius II

As the Ottoman Empire gained greater power the Muslim religion took hold on the fringes of Europe, and the Catholic Church was only able to drum up minimal support for crusading armies. The defeat of the Byzantine Empire did little to weaken the popularity of the Orthodox religion, and the Protestant Reformation spread through Europe shortly after the pope's reign ended. Pope Pius II supported Vlad Dracula's incursions into Ottoman territory and his heroic efforts to repel Mehmed the Conqueror's retaliatory invasion of Wallachia.

Pius is remembered more for his role as a religious leader than for his abilities as a ruler and statesman.

Divinatory meaning: holiness, religion and mercy. There is an element of authority in The Hierophant from which is derived the interpretation of captivity or marriage: a member of a specific religion is tied to it on both a physical level and a spiritual plane.

One portrait of Pius shows him sitting in a fortress pointing the way towards the Ottoman Empire, but there are no soldiers or pilgrims present to follow his command. The spirit of the believer is their own, and they may decide to follow a leader or to lead themselves on the spiritual course. The bondage presented by The Hierophant is one entered into willingly and openly and not necessarily for the worse.

VI. THE LOVERS

Vlad and his wife

Vlad Dracula's second wife was Justina Szilágyi, a Hungarian noblewoman; they were married for just three years, from 1474 to 1477.

Vlad had numerous mistresses and two marriages that were matters of political convenience intended to secure loyalty and support. His wives must have pleased him to some extent or they probably would have found themselves impaled on a stake. Vlad's first wife married him before he regained his throne, when his political position was still precarious, and bore him three children.

Divinatory meaning: passion, love and attraction. The Lovers card can represent a specific couple or the general positive feelings of love. Vlad and his wife are shown holding hands while standing upon the battlements of a castle. Their foundation is strong, not vulnerable to attack, but in the distance stand Turkish archers ever ready to send their arrows to end the blissful union.

No matter how strong a relationship may seem, they are vulnerable to outside influence that can come in many forms: a change of location or job status, the introduction of a third party or an internal change of heart. While The Lovers card represents a celebration of love, it should also serve as a warning to remain vigilant against potential intrusions into bliss. When partners are prepared to face challenges together the union will remain solid.

VII. THE CHARIOT

Vlad's army repelling the Turks

In the mid-1400s Wallachia was in constant political and armed tension with its neighbours as it tried to retain its status as an independent nation. A large part of this effort required an annual tribute to the dominant force in the region, the Ottoman Empire. Vlad Dracula decided to strengthen Wallachia's bond with Hungary and stopped recognising Ottoman rule over his nation.

The Turkish army was busy fighting battles and the tribute was not enforced for several years. Sensing a weakness in Mehmed II, Vlad crossed the Danube River to attack Ottoman positions and occupy their territory. Despite the overwhelming forces against him, Vlad Dracula's unconventional warfare tactics allowed him to repel the Ottoman invaders. Due to the very nature of the time in which he lived, Vlad was a military man. In order to retain any semblance of sovereign independence the countries of this era had to be willing to pay for the privilege or to fight potential oppressors. Vlad was smart enough to avoid conflict until the moment was right to strike, and had it not been for the changing political situation resulting in a Hungarian betrayal he might have been able to hold off future Ottoman incursions into Europe on the strength of his own reputation.

Divinatory meaning: war, revenge, troubles and conquest. It can be conflict that will be faced in the future, that has already occurred or that will be overcome, but conflicts are an inevitable part of life. The traditional image for The Chariot is a warrior crowned in victory riding a chariot of war but, although a positive image, The Chariot represents a conflict where victory is possible but not assured. Having a false sense of superiority can be fatal to a leader undertaking a large expedition.

Your future events probably won't involve physical combat, but each conflict does require its own unique solution. If the Suit of Coins is nearby it may be a work conflict, while if the Suit of Cups, The Lovers or The Empress are nearby it may be a relationship conflict. Be creative and employ any existing resources you have to force a larger army to retreat.

If The Chariot appears in your future it indicates a battle is on the horizon, although it's one you'll be prepared to face: there are no sneak attacks or betrayals present in the meaning of this card. Any challenge that arises will be a fair fight and your odds of victory are outstanding.

VIII. STRENGTH

'Your whole being belongs to hell!'

Vlad ordered three Catholic monks, Jacob, Michael and Hans, to be brought before him. He showed the monks the numerous bodies impaled upon stakes around his palace and asked all three what they thought of his method of keeping order. The first two monks attempted to answer diplomatically but Brother Hans unleashed a long tirade, decrying the viciousness of the practice.

He said: 'Because of the blood you have spilled on this earth, all will rise before God and His kingdom demanding vengeance. You foolish madman and senseless, unhearing tyrant, your whole being belongs to hell!' Enraged, Vlad strangled the monk with his bare hands and stomped on his head until he was dead. Vlad was a powerful man both in terms of his authority as a ruler and his actual physical strength. He led his armies into battle on countless occasions and often participated in hand-to-hand combat. The spark of rage caused by hearing Brother Hans tell the truth about his activities shows that Vlad was not merely a ruler who ordered others to perform gruesome acts on his behalf but that he was more than willing to get his hands dirty to protect his honour.

Divinatory meaning: power, energy, action and courage, along with success in a venture. Most printings of the Strength card show a woman wrestling with a lion, either forcing open its mouth or forcing it closed. This visual interpretation raises the question of which being actually possesses strength: the lion is a powerful animal that can only be subdued by a woman with god-like powers or a strong man with a big stick.

You have an internal reserve of strength that may not yet have been called upon. With the right stimulation your untapped power should be allowed to come forward unrestrained by intellectual inhibitions. Strength calls upon you to be unafraid of altering your circumstances for the better.

The Strength card does not have to indicate physical strength or force but can suggest the force of your own will. Your drive to push forward and persevere is a powerful force that can sometimes be forgotten in times of struggle and overwhelming obstacles. In a reading, this card should remind you to look inward, summon your strength and meet challenges head on.

IX. THE HERMIT

Vlad imprisoned in Visegrád

After being betrayed by his brother Radu the Handsome to the Ottoman Empire, Vlad Dracula was imprisoned in the castle of Visegrád by Hungarian king Matthias Corvinus. During his 12 years of captivity he impaled rats and other small animals on sticks.

During his captivity Vlad was invited to sit in the king's court as a display of Hungarian power. Even though deprived of all authority Vlad was still a frightening and imposing force. He endeared himself to King Matthias because, in 1475 when he was released from prison, he married the king's cousin and regained the throne of Wallachia.

Divinatory meaning: treason, hidden meanings, the passage of time and alchemy. It can also indicate solitude or a person who likes to spend time alone. Vlad's impaling of the rats can be seen as him discovering and staying true to his internal guiding compass as the rats were invaders and had to be dealt with accordingly.

The Hermit is generally depicted as a lone man perched on a mountaintop or wandering through the forest holding a walking stick and a lantern. Rather than shining the light for others to see, this lantern projects a light on the individual's internal spirit. It can point to a betrayal, although The Moon more strongly indicates deception than does this card.

X. THE WHEEL OF FORTUNE

'These suffered according to their deeds.'

Two wandering Catholic monks from Hungary visited Târgoviște palace to ask for alms. They were separately given a tour of the castle and the courtyard and shown bodies impaled on stakes and broken on the wheels of carts. Vlad asked the monks if he had done well.

The first monk replied: 'You do evil by punishing without mercy, for a ruler should be merciful, and those who are on the stakes are martyrs.' He was impaled. The second monk answered: 'As ruler, you have been appointed by God to punish those who do evil and to favour those who do good, and these people who did evil have suffered according to their deeds.' He was given 50 ducats and sent on his way in a carriage of honour.

Divinatory meaning: destiny, success, the passage of time and changing fortunes. The wheel was an excruciatingly painful way to die; it was a common method of torture at the time. A victim would have their limbs attached to the spokes and, as the wheel was turned, their arms and legs would break. The Wheel of Fortune is viewed as being a positive card as it represents the constantly changing circumstances we all live with. Things do not always go your way but eventually your situation will improve, although the inverse is also true as nobody stands at the top forever.

XI. JUSTICE

Vlad as Pontius Pilate judging Christ

Around 1460 an unknown artist painted a series of panels depicting religious scenes, possibly in Vienna. The panels resided at Velenje Castle in Slovenia for many years, until they were brought to Munich to be restored in 1933.

One panel depicts Christ being held by soldiers while Pontius Pilate sits in judgement of him. Historians studying the painting discovered that the model for Pilate appears to be Vlad Dracula. The subject's crown and the physical appearance of the character closely match most contemporary depictions of Vlad, and it's likely the artist had access to the many pamphlets describing Vlad as a cruel leader being printed in German-speaking territories at that time. That the artist would select Vlad as the embodiment of hardened, rational judgement according to the letter of the law rather than the spirit of the law suggests Vlad's clever psychological implementations of justice rather than his reputation for cruelty. (The name 'Dracul' can be interpreted as 'devil' in the Romanian language.)

Vlad Dracula was a harsh and unforgiving leader who always claimed his implementation of laws was for the benefit and general welfare of the people of Wallachia. Visiting ambassadors and dignitaries were not exempted from his rule and he killed many of them for the slightest infraction.

Although he committed many crimes against humanity, Vlad was never publicly accused or put on trial for his heinous deeds. The only authorities who might have been qualified to stand in judgement over him would be the king of Hungary, the Ottoman sultan or perhaps the pope. When Vlad finally met his end it was in the heat of battle, so we are left to believe he was condemned by divine justice.

Divinatory meaning: honesty, integrity and all things connected with law. It can indicate a court case or legal issues. Justice does not always come in an expected manner and should not be confused with revenge, which falls under the domain of The Chariot. Court cases and legal proceedings rely upon the intellect and human failings of the judge and jury, along with an individual's ability to successfully argue their case.

XII. THE HANGED MAN

The wages of truth in Wallachia

In response to hearing Hans' scathing diatribe against Vlad's impalements and cruelty Vlad stomped him to death. Hans' body was hung upside down beside a church and his donkey was impaled alive beside him, which served as a warning to visitors that there was such a thing as being too truthful in Wallachia.

Divinatory meaning: wisdom, tribulations, sacrifice and prophecy. It can also represent a hidden knowledge that, when uncovered, may be unpleasant or even cause harm. Classic depictions of The Hanged Man show a man hanging by his foot with an expression of contentment on his face and a golden halo around his head. This is a person, perhaps a martyr, who has accepted their fate and the enlightenment that comes with it.

You may seek out information that makes you feel worse than you anticipated. For example, if you suspect a partner is cheating you may snoop through their personal effects only to learn they *are* cheating. Do you end the relationship or let it continue, even though it will be diminished because of the information you have?

XIII. DEATH

Vlad beheaded by the Ottomans

Although many of the details surrounding the death of Vlad Dracula remain mysterious, most accounts state that he was killed on the battlefield outside Bucharest, the modern-day capital of Romania. After his death his head was taken to Istanbul, where it was displayed on a pike at the sultan's palace.

As one of the few military leaders to have beaten back the seemingly unstoppable Ottoman army, Vlad's death helped clear the way for the unrivalled reign of the empire and created new opportunities for the people of Wallachia. Just five years later Wallachia experienced its longest uninterrupted period of prosperity and growth through the reigns of his brother and nephew, Vlad the Monk (1482–95) and Radu the Great (1495–1508).

Divinatory meaning: endings, mortality and destruction, although conversely it can also mean rebirth and creation. In mediaeval times death was seen as being inevitable, and in an era of constant warfare and widespread disease the populace of Europe was literally surrounded by it on a daily basis. Although death brings sadness, every new beginning first requires an ending. Without death there can be no life.

XIV. TEMPERANCE

A slow execution

Vlad Dracula was infamous throughout the very cruel period of mediaeval Europe for his creativity with punishments and torture. As well as killing large numbers of people, he never tired of devising new forms of torture and death for any who dared betray him.

He particularly enjoyed impaling his victims, but he would also sit victims atop rounded stakes and tie horses to each leg. The horses would slowly pull the victim's legs apart as the stake was pushed through their body cavities. Vlad apparently commanded this form of torture because he wished to savour the victim's pain and death, which could take several hours to occur.

Divinatory meaning: moderation, frugality and economy, along with communication or movement. The Temperance card lies in a difficult position in the tarot: nestled snugly between Death and The Devil. In Milton's *Paradise Lost*, death and the devil are separated by sin. Several classical artists seized on this imagery to create drawings, engravings and paintings depicting this battle.

XV. THE DEVIL

Vlad the Impaler

Vlad Dracula was generally referred to as 'Wladislaus Dragwlya', and it wasn't until after his death that he gained the sobriquet 'Vlad Țepeș' (Vlad Impaler). The earliest known reference to Vlad as the 'Impaler' was by Turkish author and court functionary Tursun Beg; in *The History of the Conqueror* Beg gives Vlad the name Kazıklı Voyvoda, or 'Impaler Lord'. It would have been easiest to refer to Vlad III as Vlad Țepeș so people would know which Vlad was being indicated.

No rulers used impalement as effectively and consistently as Vlad did. He so enjoyed watching victims suffer he has been labelled a sadist who derived sexual pleasure from the violent act.

Divinatory meaning: bondage, lust, violence, rage and unexpected failure. The devil has long been viewed as an enemy of mankind, which can lead tarot followers to conclude The Devil card is a bad omen or an indication of evil. In a broader sense it indicates bondage in the form of addiction, staying in a bad relationship, uncontrolled sexual desire or feeling stuck in a rut.

The devil exudes a raw, lustful sexuality that doesn't have to be a negative vice as it could indicate a passionate love affair. However, unlike The Lovers card this relationship would be full of passionate conflict and sex. The devil's anger and rage come from pent-up energy that must be released in some form.

XVI. THE TOWER

'Better her body rot than be led to captivity.'

Towards the end of Vlad Dracula's second reign in 1462 his Poenari castle was under siege by Ottoman troops led by his brother, Radu the Handsome. A Wallachian soldier who was secretly loyal to Vlad tied a message indicating when the final raid would occur to an arrow and shot it into a window of the castle. Vlad's first wife read the message and, believing her husband and his troops would be outnumbered, said she would 'rather have her body rot in the Arges than be led to captivity in a Turkish prison'. She threw herself off the castle to a terrible death on the cliffs below.

Although perhaps misinformed, Vlad's princess took action and regained control over her destiny rather than letting fate dictate her future.

Divinatory meaning: distress, adversity, ruin and, in some cases, movement. It is one of the few tarot cards that in any interpretation is not particularly good. Bad things happen to everyone from time to time, but with a little advance warning you can prepare yourself and possibly mitigate or prevent negative events.

An alternate meaning of The Tower is the concept of movement, especially from a home or dwelling. Changing addresses, even when it's unexpected, can be a very positive event.

XVII. THE STAR

'Watching blood flow gave him courage.'

In 1463 German poet-minstrel Michel Beheim wrote a lengthy poem entitled 'Story of a Bloodthirsty Madman Called Dracula of Wallachia' that was composed shortly after Vlad's imprisonment in Visegrád and describes his misdeeds in excruciating detail. It repeatedly emphasises that Vlad murdered people of every age and sex without discrimination.

Part of the poem describes the punishments Vlad meted out to Dan the Younger, a pretender to the throne of Wallachia, and his followers, who were captured and impaled in the woods outside the city walls of Brasov. One line in the poem describes how much Vlad enjoyed the sight of blood and human suffering, even eating bread soaked in blood; the mere sight of blood flowing from his victims provided him with courage and vitality.

Divinatory meaning: pleasure, insight, long life, beauty, privation and the balance of gain and loss. The traditional imagery depicts a nude woman pouring two vessels of water upon the ground as a radiant star shines in the night sky, which could represent the dropping of blessings from heaven or the loss of what a person already possesses, or a combination of both. True balance involves an equal distribution of profit and loss.

The Star is a card of longevity: the light of a star can reach the earth billions of years after its distant source has burned out.

XVIII. THE MOON

Vlad betrayed by the Hungarians

In December 1462 Vlad's double dealing with the Hungarians and Ottomans led to him being attacked by a large Ottoman army commanded by his brother, Radu the Handsome. Vlad sought refuge in a clifftop fortress in the southern Carpathian Mountains known to the local Germans as Königstein, or Prince's Rock. The fortress was commanded by Czech mercenary Jan Jiskra, a deputy general for King Matthias of Hungary. Matthias wanted to avoid all-out war with the massive Ottoman army so he ordered Jiskra to take Vlad prisoner. Vlad's army could only watch helplessly as their leader was captured and put into chains.

Radu assumed the throne as a vassal of Ottoman Emperor Mehmed II. Had Vlad known the fortress at Königstein was unsafe he could have conducted a campaign of guerrilla warfare against the Ottoman forces from the Wallachian wilderness.

Divinatory meaning: deception, disillusionment, trickery, danger, hidden enemies and dreams. The moon hides something that is waiting to be revealed. As the sun lights the day the moon lights the night only by reflecting the rays of the sun; therefore the moon is regarded as a false image for the face it outwardly displays is not really its own. The false light of the moon provides a path for lesser souls who have no interest in our success but wish to be by our side to watch our downfall.

XIX. THE SUN

Vlad and Radu released from captivity

In 1442 when Vlad was aged 13 years his father disobeyed the commands of the Ottoman ruler Murad II, and his sons were taken hostage and kept under house arrest in central Turkey. Although prisoners, the children were educated and raised according to their status as the children of a nobleman and not harmed. Vlad Dracul agreed to pay tribute to the Ottoman sultan and his children were released after six years in captivity.

Vlad and Radu's time as political hostages shaped them in significantly different ways. Vlad was consistently disobedient and defied his captors, developing a legendary temper, a pedantic distaste for thieves and liars and a desire to spread bloody carnage across his realm. Radu became a favourite of the sultan's son, Mehmed, who was reputed to have fallen in love with him. Upon their release Vlad claimed the throne of Wallachia and began his first reign, but Radu became a military commander and courtier in the imperial palace when Mehmed II ascended the throne in 1451.

Divinatory meaning: accomplishment, love, success, material happiness and happy marriages. The Sun card is one of the most joyful in the tarot, traditionally depicting children with expressions of tender ecstasy and playing in the bright sunlight. This can suggest a naive or child-like answer to a question, as the simplest answer is usually the best.

XX. JUDGEMENT

Vlad's father and brother murdered

While Vlad Dracula and Radu were being held hostage in Turkey, Vlad Dracul and elder brother Mircea II made peace with the Ottoman Empire and turned Wallachia into a vassal state. This act was viewed as a betrayal by John Hunyadi, the newly appointed military governor of Hungary, who invaded Wallachia and proclaimed Vladislav II as the voivode of Wallachia, thereby unseating Vlad Dracul. Mircea was captured, blinded with a hot poker and buried alive facing downwards. His father fought to the end but was finally executed in the marshes outside Bălteni.

The following year Mehmed II released Vlad Dracula and helped him fight for the throne of Wallachia. When he discovered his brother Mircea's grave it was exhumed and the body was found facing downward, lending credence to the rumours he had been buried alive. Vlad never forgave the boyars for the murder of his brother and father, and the noble class became a favourite target for his most horrific acts of cruelty. Their action inspired him to push forward in his goal to reclaim the throne of Wallachia.

Interestingly, Vlad Dracul was laid to rest on the grounds at Dealu Monastery, the same location where his rival Vladislav II would later be buried after being executed by Vlad Dracula in revenge for the murder of his father.

Divinatory meaning: awakening, atonement, a change of position, renewal and illumination. It is a card of second chances and encourages finding a new way of dealing with problems.

There may come a time when it seems as though all is lost and your fortunes have fallen; however, even those who are dead receive a second chance to make good their efforts. The traditional Judgement card shows a heavenly angel trumpeting the dead back to life, an awakening that is an internal process with the trumpet providing inspiration to act.

In a reading focused on career, Judgement often indicates a forthcoming promotion. The reader is no longer occupying their usual static position, but will now be uplifted to new heights. The allusion of rising from the grave and ascending to the heavens could mirror a person's career progression from entry-level wage earner to highly paid executive.

XXI. THE WORLD

Vlad Dracula anointed as voivode

Following Vlad Dracula's return from exile and his triumphant defeat of Vladislav II, his position as ruler of Wallachia was formalised by the noble boyars. According to Dracula scholar Matei Cazacu, the Orthodox Metropolitan gathered the nobles outside the church of Curtea de Arges and began the election process by stating: 'Your prince is dead. Whom do you wish to choose as voivode in his place?' In response, all those assembled shouted: 'We wish only Vlad, son of Voivode Vlad!' It can only be imagined how Vlad looked upon the boyars cheering his name, many of whom he sent to their deaths a few months later. He likely felt contempt for them, knowing they had turned against his father's rule and that they would turn against him if another, stronger contender for the throne emerged.

After dropping myrrh oil upon Vlad's head during the anointing ceremony the entire congregation proclaimed 'He is worthy!' three times. For Vlad Dracula, his anointing as voivode of Wallachia was the greatest moment of his life up to that point. It was the culmination of everything he had fought for and the realsation of everything he had ever wanted.

With the anointing Vlad gained divine approval for his reign and for all the actions he undertook as ruler, a major factor in his ability to remain on the throne for so long despite his horrific acts. He would always be considered the rightful ruler of Wallachia.

Divinatory meaning: perfection, recognition, fulfilment and assured success. The World has the broadest meaning of any of the tarot cards, representing success and attainment of goals but also that which is held as the most important thing in a person's life. It may also point to the movements of the solar system's planets.

Getting what you want is different from getting what you've worked for. The World indicates the culmination of your concerted efforts to achieve a desired goal, which makes it a fitting card to end the Major Arcana as it encompasses everything that came before it and encourages you to remember the start of your journey (The Fool), the friends who helped along the way (The Lovers), the challenges (The Chariot), the apparent defeat (The Tower) and the realisation that everything is going to work out (The Sun).

MINOR ARCANA

ACE OF COINS

Coin of Vlad Dracul

As vassal states of Hungary Wallachia and Transylvania required permission from the king to create coins, which was most likely why Vlad Dracula never minted his own coins when his predecessors did. Rulers of the time had control over their own mints, so they were free to devalue their own currency by using less silver and more copper or bronze to manipulate the economy as necessary.

The two coins that may be connected to Vlad Dracula would be those minted by his father and by his predecessor, Vladislav II.

They were a bronze bani 10 mm across and a silver ducat 11 mm across, both bearing the image of a dragon on one side and an eagle and cross on the other. These coins are extremely rare, with less than 10 surviving examples.

Divinatory meaning: prosperity, contentment, pleasure, financial gain and money. The Ace of Coins is considered the most favourable of all the cards in the Minor Arcana, its meaning weighing heavily towards financial and monetary matters. The Suit of Coins is connected with the classical element of earth and the idea that prosperity grows from the soil.

TWO OF COINS

Vlad Dracula and Vlad Dracul

While a hostage in the court of Hungarian king Sigismund Vlad's father received an education and introduction to courtly life. Sigismund sent Vlad Dracul to Venice to receive Byzantine Emperor John VIII, the trip inspiring Vlad to seek his fortunes in the Byzantine Empire. He spent several years in the Imperial Court of Constantinople then journeyed north to Transylvania before settling in the walled merchant city of Sighişoara. Shortly after he was summoned to Nuremberg to attend an investiture ceremony hosted by Sigismund: his induction into the Order of the Dragon.

In the mediaeval period it was customary for Balkan rulers to be identified by nicknames either personally chosen or given by chroniclers to reflect the will of the populace. Vlad became Vlad Dracul due to his membership in the Order of the Dragon, passing the knighthood on to his son, Vlad III, on his death. The addition of an 'a' to 'Dracul' signified that the name was a younger holder of it.

Divinatory meaning: finding harmony between choices, developing new projects, a helpful person, obstacles or trouble that are more imagined than real and an unwritten future with infinite possibilities leading to paralysis. The Two of Coins is a card of choices and possibilities, but it's also a card that reminds you your imagination can conjure up non-existent problems. It's important to bite the bullet and simply make a decision – for better or worse.

It was not a foregone conclusion that Vlad Dracula would succeed his father on the Wallachian throne and there were many times in his life that he had to decide who to trust and who should be an ally. He never let fear get the better of him: he weighed his choices and reached out to grab for glory.

THREE OF COINS

Saxons building the Bucharest palace

In Vlad Dracula's time Bucharest was not of particular political importance. Curtea de Arges was the official capital and Târgovişte was Vlad's primary residence; however, Bucharest was closer to the Turkish border and was an up-and-coming trade centre due to its position between Târgşor and the Danube River. Vlad built the walls surrounding Bucharest, fortified Snagov Monastery to the north and constructed a new princely palace in the centre of the city.

As Vlad placed great importance on the battlement quality he employed Saxon builders who were masters in defensive works. They were worth their weight in gold: when the Ottoman army later invaded Wallachia it pushed as far north as Târgovişte but was unable to capture Bucharest or Snagov Monastary despite possessing cannons and an army of over 150,000 soldiers.

Divinatory meaning: abilities, approval, effort, skilled labour and renown. An architect, craftsman and artist are all skilled creators of things that are beautiful, useful and profitable. The Three of Coins celebrates artisans, but specifically the kind who are able to generate money through their art. Possessing a creative skill that is desired by others is the ultimate achievement for an artist; they will be rewarded for their abilities, allowing them to prosper.

FOUR OF COINS

Vlad paying tribute to the Ottomans

The rulers of Wallachia were obligated to pay a yearly tribute, called *harac*, of 3,000 gold ducats to the Ottoman Empire's sultan, and humiliatingly Vlad was required to deliver the tribute to Murad II in person. These annual trips to Turkey served as a reminder that his failure to continue paying the tribute could result in the execution of his hostage sons.

When Mehmed II succeeded Murad he imposed a new treaty demanding 10,000 gold ducats. Vlad Dracula was in a difficult position: as a new ruler he wanted to run Wallachia the best way possible, however, he was hindered by the money being drained from his treasury every year. There is a sense of greediness in both Sultan Mehmed demanding an exorbitant sum from his vassal but also in Vlad, who actually raised taxes on his citizens once he stopped paying the Ottoman tribute. It seems the 10,000 ducats he was saving wasn't enough to meet his demands for building fortifications and maintaining his army.

After two years the Ottoman army attacked a Wallachian border town as part of their larger war against Hungary's territory in Serbia, and Vlad used the treaty violation as an excuse to stop paying tribute. This led to his downfall, as the sultan launched a full-scale invasion of Wallachia in an attempt to collect the overdue debt.

Divinatory meaning: lack of generosity, greed, miserliness and matters of inheritance. The Four of Coins reveals the negative aspects of money and material possessions, such as greedy children waiting to get their inheritance. There is much desire tied up in the Four of Coins; specifically, earthly desires for material things. It may also point to devious secrets and evil thoughts.

Clinging to your material possessions can weigh you down in the long run. Consider what you really need and what might be best left behind or leveraged in some way to benefit your future situation. A hoarder gains nothing from their closet full of collectables, but by unburdening themselves and giving some to charity or selling it outright they will have increased living space and money in their pocket.

FIVE OF COINS

Vlad attacking foraging Ottoman soldiers

When Mehmed invaded Wallachia Vlad began a strategic retreat into the country, burning crops, destroying cities, poisoning the wells, leaving diseased bodies on the road and laying waste to everything in his path. The Ottomans became desperate for food, and were exhausted and in a constant state of thirst. Vlad refused to give the enemy any rest, preventing them from eating or sleeping.

Divinatory meaning: destitution, poor health, despair, loneliness and Bohemian habits bred by carelessness or travel. This is the darkest card of the Suit of Coins, as it represents a lack of money and the negative feelings that accompany a position of poverty. The traditional image is one of wandering beggars trudging through the snow. The Five of Coins can have a connection to travel, although it might be travel that causes financial difficulties such as a holiday that is taken on credit.

Sometimes life kicks you when you're down, whether it's an unpaid debt or an obstacle that can only be solved by money. And, like Vlad's raiding parties, sometimes the attacker suddenly appears to take another swing while you're trying to gather some wild berries for sustenance. Remember there are always options, even if it means temporarily retreating to fight another day.

SIX OF COINS

Wealthy Saxon merchants of Transylvania

Germans (or Saxons) began colonising Transylvania in the 1100s as part of a wider trend of migration from the more populous cities in central Europe to the wild mountains and forests of eastern Europe. By the 1200s they were a privileged class that exercised semi-autonomous government over their own territories.

In the fortified city of Sighişoara, the birthplace of Vlad Dracula, 14 towers were placed in a defensive circle around the walls to protect the city against attacks from invaders. Due to the advanced construction techniques utilised by the Saxon builders, an army could not gain access to the city simply by taking one tower or scaling one section of the wall. The main gates, which had heavy doors with layers of defences such as arrow slits and sluices to drop hot oil on invaders, were the only way to access the city. The fact that the towers and walls are still standing nearly 600 years later is a testament to the importance the merchants placed upon these defences.

Divinatory meaning: prosperity, philanthropy, gifts and gratification. There is much goodwill connected with the Six of Coins, a card of financial success and of good works associated with the money that was gained. It indicates someone who has found prosperity and is willing to share it with others as presents or donations.

SEVEN OF COINS

Boyars forced to build Castle Dracula

By 1457 Vlad Dracula had retaken the Wallachian throne and wanted to purge himself of those boyars who had fought against him. The heads of the families were assembled in a meeting hall and asked how many princes had ruled over the land during their lifetimes; there had been 15 different rulers of Wallachia throughout the era.

Vlad told the boyars they had had many princes because of their shameful intrigue. He ordered the 50 heads of the boyar families to be impaled on stakes outside the palace while his soldiers rounded up the remaining men, women and children, who were marched to Poenari Castle and forced to work as slave labourers on its construction. They worked day and night until their clothes rotted off their bodies, and were then forced to continue working naked.

Divinatory meaning: development, re-evaluation, effort, hard work and business altercations or quarrels. The Seven of Coins is a card about action, or accomplishing things at any cost and with great effort. This action involves requiring or receiving assistance from outside sources, which can lead to arguments about money or business decisions. It can also represent looking back on your past efforts and evaluating the fruits of your labour.

EIGHT OF COINS

'I have found an extra ducat.'

A Florence merchant stopped in Târgovişte to rest. He asked Vlad Dracula to post a guard by his cart, which was filled with merchandise and gold, but the following morning when the merchant checked his cart he found that 160 gold ducats had been stolen.

Vlad commanded that the thief be sought out and captured, at the same time secretly ordering his treasurer to replace the stolen bag of gold but to add one extra coin. The merchant counted the returned gold and said to Vlad: 'I have found all my money, only with an extra ducat.' Vlad said to the merchant: 'If you had not returned the extra ducat I would have impaled you alongside the thief.'

Divinatory meaning: money, learning, trade and material prudence. As the Eight of Coins traditionally bears the image of a craftsman working diligently to create pentacles, which will bring him prosperity, it is often interpreted as being connected to working in a craft or trade although there is a stronger case for that connection in the Three of Coins. While working at a craft could certainly bring financial stability, the concept of prudence is dominant in this card. Prudence and honesty are important principles when dealing with money, for nothing can destroy relationships as quickly as financial issues.

NINE OF COINS

'A farmer must cut the weeds and roots.'

Brother Hans noted that not only were men put upon the impalement stake but also women (some pregnant) and children. He could see no rationale for such evil punishments and asked Vlad why he was so vicious. Vlad explained: 'When a farmer wishes to clear the ground for plowing, he must not only cut thorns and weeds that have grown up but also clear out their roots. In these little children I would have created the gravest enemies when, as adults, they grew to avenge their fathers.'

Wallachia was a country of rich farmland heavily populated by peasant farmers. The strength of the nation rested on both Saxon merchants and agricultural production, and although Vlad had great appreciation for the peasants he despised those who were weak or lazy. If he dug out the roots early enough he could enjoy safety and success in the coming years.

Divinatory meaning: solitude, well-being, green thumbs and self-satisfaction. The Nine of Coins has many connections with agriculture and growth and success in general, and also to material well-being or a sense of safety in the context of having a material safety net. The traditional imagery of the Nine of Coins is a woman in the garden of an English manor holding a bird on her hand, indicating that the work of planting and maintaining the garden has already been finished and she may now enjoy the rewards.

TEN OF COINS

Vlad's hidden treasure

Snagov Monastery, the probable location of Vlad's burial tomb, is located on an island in the centre of a lake a short distance from Bucharest. Towards the end of his final reign, Vlad ordered his servants to seal the bulk of his gold in giant barrels that were sunk into the lake. Vlad then had the servants put to death so they could not reveal the location of the treasure.

High out of reach of an invading army, Poenari Castle would have been an even more secure location for Vlad's gold; historians believe there could still be a hidden vault in the mountain fortress containing a hoard of riches. One legend says that on certain nights the castle glows with an eerie golden flame that indicates the location of the buried treasure to any adventurer brave enough to seek it out.

Divinatory meaning: wealth, property, stability, gain and riches. This Ten of Coins deals exclusively with wealth and property, representing the creation of opportunities to accumulate money or find financial success. It indicates the possession of wealth without drawbacks, hardship or danger, rather only financial gain and stability.

Vlad the Monk, Vlad Dracula's brother

PAGE OF COINS

Vlad the Monk, Vlad Dracula's brother

Vlad Călugărul (Romanian for 'monk') was the second son of Vlad Dracul but the last of his brothers to ascend the throne. His reign as voivode from 1482 to 1495 was one of the longest in Wallachia during the mediaeval period. An Orthodox priest at Snagov Monastery, he was known among his fellow monks by the priestly name of Brother Pahomie.

Vlad Călugărul eventually became abbot of the island fortress but was defrocked for unknown reasons in 1466. He settled in the Transylvania town of Sibiu and married Rada Smaranda. In 1482, at almost 60 years of age, he was installed as voivode by Stephen III of Moldavia. After becoming ruler Vlad took a new wife, Maria Palaiologina, the wife of the voivode he had displaced. He was a kind ruler who successfully balanced the needs of his own people and the foreign powers he served, and was one of the few voivodes to die without being overthrown.

Divinatory meaning: kindness, new ideas, rule and management and a dark youth, young officer or soldier. The Page of Coins is a kind young man who brings new ideas along with a love of knowledge, a person who enjoys cultivating an intellectual relationship and who will engage in romance in a gentle fashion. There are many honourable offices in this card, including those of civil service, commerce or writing or selling books.

KNIGHT OF COINS

Mihnea the Bad, Vlad's eldest son

Although much of his early life is the subject of debate among scholars, Mihnea was most likely born while his father was living in exile after being deposed in 1448. As a child he was a hostage to the Ottoman Empire, where he was raised and educated in the court of Mehmed II. After his father was chased off the throne by Radu the Handsome, Mihnea fled Ottoman captivity and spent the next 30 years serving in the court of the kings of Hungary. In 1494 Mihnea settled in Sibiu, and undertook a plot to persuade the boyars to support his candidacy to become the next voivode. When Vlad the Monk's son, Radu the Great, ascended the throne Mihnea was chased out of Sibiu, but in May 1508 following Radu's death Mihnea was finally successful at persuading the noble families of Wallachia to bring him to the throne.

He exacted a cruel and bloody revenge upon the boyars who had failed to support him in the past: raping and pillaging through the countryside, burning entire villages, cutting the noses and ears off priests, burning abbots alive in their monasteries and raping noble family members. He devoted himself to robbing and confiscating goods and money from the traders and nobles of Wallachia, behaviour that earned him the nickname 'Mihnea the Bad'; he was eventually murdered by Serbian nobles.

Divinatory meaning: dull outlook, usefulness, help, endurance and strength. The Knight of Coins is a card representing slow but assured assistance. There may be an inheritance or some other monetary gain, but it will not come by the expected route. The knight could be a person who will provide financial resources or temporary help in the form of a loan.

Mihnea the Bad continued his father's legacy in more ways than one: he wanted desperately to retake the throne from his uncle and his cousin but lacked the political acumen and charm necessary to unite the noble families of Wallachia behind him. However, despite waiting over 20 years after the death of his father, Mihnea did eventually succeed in reclaiming his birthright as voivode. His reign was bloody and might have been more profitable for him had he not focused his efforts entirely on robbing his own people.

QUEEN OF COINS

Justina Szilágyi, Vlad's second wife

Justina Szilágyi, King Matthias' cousin, spent her life in marriages arranged without her consent. As a lower-ranking noblewoman whose father died while she was still young, she was an easy political pawn who could be moved around to secure the loyalty of various landowners. Her first marriage to a Hungarian nobleman was arranged by the king in order to secure an exchange of strategic land for estates in Transylvania. She was 25 when he died and she returned to Hungary.

In 1474 Matthias arranged for Justina to marry Vlad Dracula, who was living in the city of Buda as a captive guest of the king. Following their marriage Vlad began to plot his return to the throne of Wallachia by courting the boyars, the Saxons and the merchants of Brasov. He successfully led an invasion of Wallachia and was once again recognised as voivode. Immediately after Vlad's death Justina was married to Paul Suki under orders from Matthias. She died in 1497.

Divinatory meaning: generosity, reliability, melancholy, presents from a rich relative, a dark woman who is helpful. The Queen of Coins is an intelligent woman able to contemplate and comprehend her place in the world and how she may best be of use in the larger workings around her. As a ruler of the earthly Suit of Coins she will protect and grow material wealth and financial success.

KING OF COINS

Dan III forced to dig his own grave

Dan the Younger was the brother of Vladislav II, the man responsible for murdering Vlad Dracul in 1447 and seizing the throne of Wallachia. When Vladislav was executed by Vlad Dracula in 1456, Dan became one of several rival claimants to the title of voivode. For four years he attempted to lead an insurrection against Vlad's rule, even going so far as to have himself proclaimed voivode Dan III of Wallachia by the boyars of Brasov.

In 1460 Vlad finally caught Dan outside the city walls of Brasov. He ordered Dan to dig his own grave then, after the grave was finished, beheaded Dan and placed him in the hole. Dan's followers were impaled in a massive display of horror at the base of Tâmpa Hill. This was one of the first incidents of Vlad's use of mass impalement to send a clear message to any other potential claimants to the throne of Wallachia.

Divinatory meaning: steadiness, valour and an aptitude for business. The King of Coins (or Pentacles) does not solely represent money or even finances, but has more to do with economy or business in general. It represents the four signs mixed together in a person and shows a great deal of nobility, integrity and honesty. There may be a connection to vanity and some self-centredness in a person identified by this card, but it is not of an evil or negative type.

ACE OF CUPS

Vlad's golden chalice

Vlad Dracula's unique logic concerning morality and justice is illustrated by the story of his golden chalice. He set an elaborate gold cup beside a spring water fountain along the road leading into Târgovişte; it was free for anyone to drink from the fountain during their travels. Despite the value of the golden chalice it was never stolen, as everyone in the land feared the reprisals for stealing from the cup's owner. This action simultaneously demonstrates Vlad Dracula's generosity, confidence and ferocity toward anyone who dared venture into his realm.

Divinatory meaning: good health, joy, beauty, love and inflexible will or law. The Ace of Cups is closely connected with Catholic concepts of holiness and divine law. In this card, the flowing blood of Christ is combined with the holy water stoup or even the baptismal font in a church, thus there is an element of salvation and protection, and a pouring out of blessings upon the faithful. As the primary card of the water element, movement can also be indicated.

TWO OF CUPS

Vlad's promises to Hungary and Turkey

As voivode of Wallachia, Vlad Dracula was forced to cater to the demands of Hungary – ruled by a Catholic monarch with political ties throughout Europe – and the Ottoman Empire – ruled by a Muslim monarch with one of the most powerful armies in the world and control over lucrative trade routes. It is testament to Vlad Dracula's political acumen and interpersonal charm that he was able to negotiate with these two competing powers.

Vlad was additionally burdened by the pressures of competing religions. Although not a Catholic, he was able to convince Hungary's King Matthias that he was a servant of God who would answer the call to fight as a member of the Christian brotherhood. Sultan Mehmed II, however, was less concerned with Vlad's religion than with his treatment and protection of Muslim merchants, soldiers and dignitaries travelling through Wallachia. As his rule over his own people became more secure, Vlad chose not to honour the promises he made to his fellow monarchs and was removed from the throne as a result.

Divinatory meaning: love, friendship, affinity, union and cooperation. The Two of Cups relates to affection and love between two persons, specifically romantic love or close friendship. There is cooperation and partnership between two people and a joining together of their energies for the betterment of both.

THREE OF CUPS

Vlad and the Benedictine monks

Three Benedictine monks were granted refuge in Wallachia after being expelled from their monastery in Slovenia. As part of their monastic vows they walked barefoot and lived simple lives collecting alms from the local populace. When Vlad Dracula showed them the horrors of his torture and asked them what they thought of his punishment methods, only one was wise enough to tell Vlad what he wanted to hear. The two honest monks were swiftly impaled but Brother Jacob was sent on his way, relating the stories of Vlad's cruelty to the rest of Europe. His first-hand tales of terror served as the basis for later pamphlets and poems about Vlad Dracula that became Europe's first horror stories.

Divinatory meaning: the conclusion of any matter, perfection, merriment, unexpected advancement, hospitality and discovery. The Three of Cups, which traditionally depicts three women raising cups aloft in celebration, represents happiness and success. This card is connected with good health and positive business advancement, especially when there is a third party that will provide advancement or help move an enterprise forward.

FOUR OF CUPS

The beggars' feast

Vlad Dracula laid out all manner of food and drink and invited the poor, ill and itinerant from throughout Wallachia to the feast. After they had finished he asked them if there was anything else they wanted. When they told him they had all they desired, Vlad ordered the doors of the barn locked and the entire structure set on fire; 600 people were burned alive in the blaze. When asked why he had done this deed, Vlad replied: 'Now there shall be no more poor in my country, and all will be rich.'

Divinatory meaning: weariness, aversion, disgust, re-evaluation and redemption. The Four of Cups indicates unhappiness or dissatisfaction, suggesting someone who is weary with the world and has everything they have asked for but is still not happy with the result. This is a condition of always wanting more, always striving toward the next thing and not being content. It is also a card of blended pleasure: there may be positive outcomes but that positivity will not be appreciated.

FIVE OF CUPS

'No one will be poor in my realm.'

An alternative telling of the beggars' feast story suggests that those who were locked in the barn were not the poor and sick but lazy peasants from Wallachia who lived off public welfare. Vlad burned them alive so they would no longer be a burden on his country and so they would no longer have to worry about being poor or sick because they were dead.

Divinatory meaning: loss, regret and sorrow. Although sorrow is attached to the Five of Cups it is not all-consuming loss although it can be powerful to whoever is affected by it. In traditional imagery a man in a dark cloak has three cups spilled but two cups remaining upright and full. The Five of Cups can also relate to family matters or marriage issues but these are not exclusively negative; they will be mixed. The card is especially indicative of inheritance.

SIX OF CUPS

Romanians honouring Vlad Dracula

Although often viewed as a monstrous figure in the Western world, Vlad Dracula has long been considered a national hero of Romania. He prevented the country from falling into the hands of the Ottoman Empire and the kingdom of Hungary, helping to maintain the national identity of modern Romanians. His popularity is evident throughout Romania in the many statues dedicated to him.

One bust in the historic old town centre of Bucharest is among the ruins of the Curtea Veche, which was constructed by Vlad Dracula in 1459 to strengthen the town's defences. The prominence of this statue in the heart of the Romanian capital's bustling tourist centre demonstrates the nation's pride in their historical hero, who protected the country's independence at the tip of a spear. Part of Vlad's enduring legacy is the fact that Bram Stoker appropriated the name 'Dracula' for his vampire and wrote such a compelling story making the name synonymous with evil power.

Divinatory meaning: good memories and health, happiness, joy of celebration and events from the past coming to prominence again. The simple happiness inherent in the Six of Cups might come as the remembering of a pleasant thought from childhood. The traditional image of the Six of Cups shows children in a garden, which can indicate friendship, country life and sharing.

SEVEN OF CUPS

Serving soup from a boiled thief

One of the most unusual stories about Vlad relates to his punishment of a gypsy thief. The thief's clan asked Vlad for their friend's release, and he agreed to release the thief on the condition that the gypsy clan hang the criminal. The gypsies explained that theft was not a capital offence and that the Holy Roman emperor had commanded that no gypsy could be executed by hanging. Vlad had the thief thrown into a large cauldron and boiled alive, then he forced the unfortunate man's comrades to consume the resulting soup. Under threat of a death more horrible than the one they had just witnessed, the gypsy clan was compelled to consume not only the broth but also the flesh and softened bones of the thief.

Vlad's improvised punishment was inventive and, by forcing the gypsies to eat the boiled man's flesh, he made it clear that his commands were not to be questioned.

Divinatory meaning: imagination, illusion and feeling directionless. This card is about illusion and unusual fantasies that can never come to fruition. The Seven of Cups symbolises images that come and go in a passing fancy.

EIGHT OF CUPS

Saxon traitors boiled alive

Vlad Dracula was constantly at odds with the various groups vying for power in his realm, and perhaps none were so conversely loved and hated as the Saxons. Vlad desperately needed them to maintain the treasury and build his defensive structures, but their German heritage and desire for independence made them dangerous enemies whenever they united against his rule.

Vlad once seized 600 merchants, confiscated their goods and money and had them impaled and boiled alive in a special cauldron he had constructed with a wooden lid containing a hole in the top. As the cauldron was heated over a fire Vlad could enjoy the sight of their pained, terrified faces while savouring the chorus of screams.

Divinatory meaning: disappointment, abandonment, unhappiness and abandoned success. The Eight of Cups traditionally depicts a man walking away from a stack of cups he has built, the implication being he is not satisfied with his work and has abandoned it. It may be that the work has not provided the expected result, or that the work was not as important as was originally thought. In this respect the Eight of Cups can be considered a card of revelation and not necessarily of misery. In general the card relates to the end of an enterprise such as a business venture or a family situation.

NINE OF CUPS

Rhodes celebrating Vlad's victories

In 1462 Mehmed II led one of the largest armies ever assembled into Wallachia to force Vlad Dracula to pay the tribute he owed as a vassal of the Ottoman Empire. Against overwhelming odds and using terror tactics and guerrilla warfare, Vlad forced the Ottomans into a strategic retreat and prevented Wallachia from being overrun.

The news of Vlad's triumph was hailed as a victory of Christianity over Islam. Because of Vlad's victory the governor of Rhodes, Piero Raimondo Zacosta, ordered his army to begin repairing the island's defences and stockpile enough wheat and wine for a two-year siege; however, the Ottoman fleet instead invaded the island of Lesbos. When the Ottoman assault on Rhodes finally occurred eight years later, the Knights Hospitaller were ready and successfully won their own victory against the sultan.

Divinatory meaning: contentment, victory and success. The Nine of Cups represents a joyous feast that has been earned. Not only is the past celebrated, but the present offers contentment and still more benefit will be found in the future. It also indicates hopes and dreams made real by a person's own power. The Nine of Cups has connections with parties, celebrations and military victories.

TEN OF CUPS

Vlad Dracula and his family

Vlad Dracula had three sons. The eldest, Mihnea, was a hostage to the Ottoman court. The second son, Mircea, died at age 18 while serving Bishop John Filipec, an influential adviser to Hungary's King Matthias. The third son, Vlad Drakulya de Sintești, made a claim for the Wallachian throne but was chastised by Matthias and ordered to leave Wallachia. Shortly after this ignominious development Vlad Drakulya died, leaving Mihnea the Bad free to claim the throne.

Vlad must have had some influence over his children and their upbringing: the oldest son became an over-achiever, the middle son rebelled against his father by working for a Catholic bishop and the youngest child tried to be the same strong leader his father was but fell short and died of shame.

Divinatory meaning: happiness and the connections of human love and friendship. The Ten of Cups radiates family, representing the home, a city and any place where people gather together to enjoy one another's company. It may also indicate physical ownership of a home or moving into an abode. Happiness and a feeling of contentment are most prevalent in this card, especially the sensation of returning to your own home after a long time away or at the end of a long day.

PAGE OF CUPS

Young Vlad watching executions

The pale yellow house where Vlad Dracula was born lies in the shadow of a great clock tower. Historians have painted a romantic picture of young Vlad sitting in his bedroom watching as prisoners were led through the city square on their way to being executed at the Jewellers' Tower, and even peeking into their prison cells through iron-barred windows.

Vlad's father was a respected leader in the city and may have been responsible for condemning some criminals to death, so it's quite possible his children attended the executions as it was a common practice in those days. Vlad Dracula had enough exposure to violent acts in his youth to help shape his character as an adult. Witnessing his father's role in the cold execution of justice impressed upon young Vlad the importance of maintaining law and order at any cost to serve the greater good of the community.

Divinatory meaning: a fair young man or studious youth, dreams and fantasies. The Page of Cups represents an intellectual dreamer with the tools to bring those dreams to life. The person indicated by this card will always be a friend, although they may be transitory or an impermanent presence. This card can also relate to meditation and reflection upon that which has already been learned.

Radu the Handsome, Vlad's brother

KNIGHT OF CUPS

Radu the Handsome, Vlad's brother

The third son born to Vlad Dracul, Radu served with Vlad Dracula as a hostage in the court of the Ottoman Empire. Radu was exposed exclusively to Islamic culture and educated in the traditional style of the Turkish noble class. When he left captivity he chose to remain in the service of Sultan Murad II due to his close friendship with the sultan's son, Mehmed, and because he felt he would have more chances for success and advancement by serving the sultan.

Radu was christened the 'Handsome' because his physical appearance was so striking. He participated in the final assault on Constantinople and contributed to the fall of the Byzantine Empire then, in 1462, he took part in a full-scale invasion of Wallachia that intended to force Vlad Dracula to submit to Ottoman rule. He was rewarded for fighting against his brother by being proclaimed voivode of Wallachia, but died in 1475 shortly after his final overthrow.

Oddly enough, the 15th-century author William Wey believed that Vlad Dracula captured and murdered Radu the Handsome in the aftermath of the night attack on Târgovişte. He stated: 'Vlad himself met his brother and stabbed him with a spear in his throat. And so he stuck the spear to which his brother hung with his body against the sun.' This certainly fits the description of Vlad's typical style of retribution against his enemies – impaling them and putting their body on public display to rot in the sun. However, as Radu is known to have been alive long after that battle, Wey must have been merely relating a rumour.

Divinatory meaning: romance, emotion, advances, proposition, invitation and incitement. The Knight of Cups is a graceful, passive figure. The card is tied closely to sensations such as love or emotions that are felt but perhaps not expressed, suggesting harmless secrets of the heart to be revealed. At its core the Knight of Cups represents a romantic lover who is never standing still but is constantly moving towards the object of desire. A lover must be careful to be faithful to their partners, otherwise they will find themselves alone.

QUEEN OF CUPS

Princess Maria Voichița of Moldavia

Vlad Dracula's niece, Maria Voichița, daughter of Radu the Handsome, became a highly influential figure in Wallachian–Moldavian relations. Little is known of her life before 1473, when she and her mother were captured by the Moldavian army. Radu fled the battle and all his possessions were plundered by the invaders; he never saw his wife or daughter again.

Although at the time in a marriage of political convenience with his second wife, nothing could quell Prince Stephen's desire for the daughter of his adversary; he waited one year after his wife's death to marry Maria. She took an active role in the governing of Moldavia and was an extremely influential figure in the royal court. Maria's beauty never faded, and there is much evidence of the prince's love for her in the northern Romanian monasteries.

Divinatory meaning: a good, fair woman who is honest and devoted, a perfect spouse and a good mother. The Queen of Cups is a woman who sees and acts upon the visions in the murky water of her chalice; she can fulfil the needs of both her spouse and her children. This card may also indicate a woman of authority or wisdom whose advice should be heeded in certain circumstances, along with a desire to make a name for yourself in the world and to draw attention to your abilities.

KING OF CUPS

Prince Stephen III of Moldavia

The turbulent political situation in mediaeval Moldavia was brought to an end with the rise of Prince Stephen III, known also as Stephen the Great. He was 10 years younger than Vlad Dracula but the future rulers forged a close bond while Vlad was preparing his return to the throne and Stephen was in training to become a monarch himself. When he took the throne in 1457 he kept the Ottoman Empire happy by paying their required tribute, which would ultimately lead to a break between the two monarchs.

Stephen became a hated adversary of the Ottomans and stopped paying the tribute. However, his continued military victories against the empire caused financial difficulties, so he convinced the Hungarian king to release Vlad from imprisonment to help him reacquire the throne of Wallachia. The Ottomans invaded Wallachia in 1477 and assassinated Vlad. Stephen ruled Moldavia and defended it from Ottoman and Polish attacks for the next 30 years, eventually dying from the complications of gangrene. Stephen's energy, enthusiasm and faithfulness to his friends made him a powerful leader; he is still celebrated today.

Divinatory meaning: a fair man who is good with business and the law, kindness, willingness, friendship, honesty, integrity and imagination. The King of Cups can represent a person who has an exuberant personality, but it will always be someone who is helpful and always available when called upon. The presence of water in the Suit of Cups can indicate a person whose loyalty shifts, although not with evil intent. This card is also connected with business promotion and financial gain, often through the help of someone with great authority.

Prince Stephen III is rightly remembered as a great ruler. He successfully maintained Moldavia's independence and repeatedly tried to expand his country's borders while simultaneously defending those same borders against his adversaries. Stephen was a true friend to Vlad Dracula, although they had their differences at times; he not only ousted Radu the Handsome from the throne, but actually provided a protective personal guard for Vlad in his time of need. Stephen's energy, enthusiasm and faithfulness to his friends is part of what made him such a powerful leader and a historical figure who is still celebrated today.

ACE OF STAKES

Impaling stake

The earliest confirmed use of impalement was in ancient Mesopotamia, as a punishment for spousal murder in adultery cases. It was used throughout the centuries in numerous Middle Eastern cultures. In mediaeval Europe and the Ottoman Empire impalement was primarily utilised as punishment for adultery, war-time crimes and robbery, the intention being to make the accused suffer for what they had done and to serve as a potent warning against future offences.

With impalement, the wooden stake must first be selected and prepared then mounted deeply in the ground so it will not tip over with the body's weight. The condemned person must be hoisted upon the stake, and someone must stand nearby to ensure they actually die from the wound.

Divinatory meaning: creation, invention, enterprise and the beginning of a new business. The Ace of Stakes (or Wands) is traditionally depicted as a wand appearing from a puff of smoke, possibly symbolising air. However, in truth it symbolises fire, which makes perfect sense as the sticks are piled together to serve as fuel to propel an enterprise forward. At its core the Stakes suit represents intuition and activity, with the ace being the embodiment of those things. What will provide the spark that drives you forward to success?

TWO OF STAKES

The deceit of Hamza and Katabolinos

In early 1462 Vlad Dracula refused to pay the required tribute to the Ottomans, failed to give personal homage to Mehmed II and delayed the conscription of 500 young Wallachian men for the Ottoman army's elite janissary corps. Mehmed had the skilled Greek diplomat and his most capable administrator, Thomas Katabolinos, escort Vlad to the Ottoman capital to discuss the way to move forward. Hamza Bey, a celebrated admiral of the Ottoman navy and governor of the Nicopolis region, would serve as temporary military protector of Wallachia while Vlad was absent.

Vlad, however, had already determined he would not negotiate in person with the sultan, and Katabolinos was surprised to find him with a fully armed escort. When Hamza and his troops descended Vlad was ready for them; the majority of the enemy soldiers and diplomats were killed or captured. Vlad ordered Hamza and Katabolinos to be impaled, taking special care to hoist Hamza upon the highest stake in a mocking show of respect. They were the last envoys sent by Sultan Mehmed to Vlad Dracula.

Divinatory meaning: courage, patience, melancholy over responsibilities, fortune and riches. The Two of Stakes is a challenging card with many meanings, in general symbolising the kind of melancholy that can accompany great success and the intense responsibility that comes with it. Historical interpretations of the card relate it to Alexander the Great looking over his vast domain and realising there were no more worlds to conquer, that he was now required to govern his possessions instead of enjoying the sting of battle. In that respect the Two of Stakes can indicate personal growth or moving upward from one level to another.

THREE OF STAKES

Dracula's dreadful and curious things

'In the year of Our Lord 1456 Dracula did many dreadful and curious things': so begins the first line of a pamphlet printed in 1488. The pamphlet was essentially a long list of Vlad Dracula's cruel acts and was intended to shock and frighten readers.

Vlad had many different ways of dealing with the challenges that occurred during his life, and although impalement was his favourite there were many other dreadful methods. His ability to adapt to nearly any situation and overcome various obstacles was a huge part of his success as a ruler and contributed to the longevity of his legend, although his tactics secured his place in the annals of human history as one of the cruellest tyrants to ever live.

Divinatory meaning: strength, enterprise, success in business, cooperation and a good partnership. The Three of Stakes represents established strength and success already being enjoyed. It is a card of commerce that can indicate a cooperative effort that will reap financial rewards. Even when this card is in the reversed position, it still suggests a very positive outcome.

FOUR OF STAKES

The courtyard of Târgovişte Palace

Târgovişte was constructed in the early 1400s but not made the official capital of Wallachia until 1431. Vlad Dracula primarily ruled from Târgovişte Palace but utilised Poenari Castle as his primary fortress whenever his situation became precarious.

Due to instability Vlad greatly fortified Târgovişte, his most lasting addition being Chindia Tower. From this tower Vlad would have had an excellent view of the surrounding countryside, allowing him to prepare for any potential attacks and observe the mass impalements that frequently occurred in the open courtyard below.

In a strange coincidence, Nicolae Ceaușescu, the brutal dictator who ruled Romania with an iron fist from 1965–89, was tried and executed in the courtyard of a military building only one mile away from Târgovişte palace.

Divinatory meaning: safe haven, peace, domestic harvest and unexpected good fortune. The Four of Stakes radiates abundance and safety, the effect of which leads inevitably to domestic happiness, harmony and future success. It does not represent domestic or home life in and of itself but as a consequence of good fortune.

FIVE OF STAKES

Wallachians fighting the Ottomans

Prior to Romania's independence in 1878 its constituent states of Wallachia, Transylvania and Moldavia were in constant conflict with the Ottoman Empire. In an effort to compel Vlad Dracula to honour the terms of his vassalage, in 1462 Mehmed II assembled around 250,000 troops to invade Wallachia. Commanding less than 30,000 men and knowing he would have to resort to drastic measures, Vlad made it impossible for the invaders to remain by burning crops, poisoning wells and arranging for peasants infected with plague to wander through the Turkish camps.

The sultan's resolve for battle was further drained by Vlad's daring night attack at Târgovişte. Disguised as a Turkish soldier, Vlad went through the camp to learn its layout then led a vicious assault after nightfall. The Wallachian cavalry ran freely among the Ottoman tents, slaying soldiers, horses and camels. Vlad was celebrated across Europe as a hero of Christianity for his miraculous battle against the Muslim invaders; it is believed 20,000 Ottoman soldiers were killed. This was the final armed conflict before the invaders were finally repelled.

Divinatory meaning: strife, competition and struggles for personal gain. The Five of Stakes symbolises the struggle for success in life. We are constantly surrounded by the challenges of daily life, and this card reminds us that victory or defeat in battle is not preordained and we should not be afraid to pour our energy into ensuring a positive outcome. With struggle comes a more satisfying success than if victory had just been handed to us on a silver platter.

SIX OF STAKES

The forest of the impaled

Although the dramatic attack against the Ottoman forces seriously weakened the resolve of the invading army to continue their campaign, encountering the forest of the impaled was the final straw that caused Mehmed to retreat from Wallachia. He marched north toward the prince's palace and was confronted by a horrifying spectacle: Vlad had ordered all captured Turkish soldiers to be impaled outside the grounds of the palace. He also emptied the jails and threw the prisoners onto stakes, and even dug up the recently deceased and had them mounted.

More than 20,000 bodies of men, women and children were hoisted aloft on stakes to rot in the summer heat, creating the illusion of a massive forest of death. It was a sight that rattled even the battle-hardened Turkish soldiers, who had committed war-time atrocities themselves. Mehmed ordered a strategic withdrawal from Wallachian territory and never again dared to lead troops against Vlad Dracula.

Divinatory meaning: leadership, good news and success. The Six of Stakes traditionally depicts a rider on horseback bearing a crown of laurels met with celebration, which can be interpreted as a messenger bringing good news and a herald of victory or a leader returning from a successful mission. The success it represents might be due to a special ability or skill, but they will come quickly.

SEVEN OF STAKES

'He placed their parts on stakes.'

Numerous historical accounts from the 1400s and 1500s describe Vlad Dracula's not only killing, maiming and impaling people but also chopping them into pieces and impaling the pieces. He was known to have done this on several specific occasions: when punishing the followers of the usurper Dan III, after attacking the border city of Nicopolis and throughout his short-lived invasion of Bulgaria. It suggests that this literal overkill of his enemies was part of his wish to terrify his enemies into submission and also prevent them from turning against him in the future.

Some historians believe Vlad's psychotic personality led him to commit bloody acts. Chroniclers from Germany, Austria and Russia all relate that Vlad butchered his victims 'like cabbage' and placed their parts on stakes.

Divinatory meaning: stiff competition, success, courage and valour. The Seven of Stakes is connected with competition that will ultimately result in victory and with courage in the face of challenges. The time and energy Vlad Dracula expended to dismember and impale victims who were already dead could suggest his overwhelming desire to be viewed as a victor who would accept no dissension from his rule.

'Arrows drove the Turks to their ships.'

EIGHT OF STAKES

'Arrows drove the Turks to their ships.'

When Mehmed II led a massive invasion of Wallachia in 1462 he wished to make a speedy strike with overwhelming force. However, as part of his scorched earth tactics Vlad had strengthened the fortresses at strategic points along the border to prevent any river crossings and left just one port open in an attempt to lure his enemies to that location and entice them to cross.

When the Turkish soldiers began to sail across the river a detachment of concealed Wallachian archers surprised them with a volley of arrows that sent them scrambling back to their boats. Radu the Handsome, commander of the janissary forces, took his men to a point several miles downstream and ordered his soldiers to cross the river at night. Radu was able to use his men as a shield to take 120 pieces of artillery across the river, which they used to disperse the archers. A beachhead was established and the rest of the Ottoman army crossed the Danube with ease.

Divinatory meaning: swiftness, great haste in an undertaking, movement and love or passion. The Eight of Stakes indicates events that are close at hand and likely to be the realisation of hopes. Through the flying arrows of love it often represents love and passion, although it might also suggest the negative side of love with the arrows of jealousy. Due to the astrological position of the card it has a strong connection to water.

NINE OF STAKES

Vlad Dracula dining among the impaled

The image of Vlad Dracula enjoying a meal amid the carnage of dozens of impaled bodies encapsulates the deeds that made the name 'Dracula' that of a villain rather than a hero. The event that inspired the woodcut was the mass impalement of the followers of Dan the Younger, a Romanian noble who tried to seize the throne of Wallachia in 1460. Vlad relished the opportunity of putting an end to Dan's political ambitions, swiftly crushing the rebellion, capturing Dan and forcing him to dig his own grave, and even impaling soldiers who had already died in battle.

The descriptions of the event contain what may be the only verified occurrence of Vlad's cannibalistic behaviour, with the original German text stating that during the execution Vlad either dipped his bread or washed his hands in the blood of his victims. Vlad's mass impalement of his enemies inspired his nickname 'the Impaler'.

Divinatory meaning: obstacles, delay, misfortune, victory, strength and revolution. The Nine of Stakes represents two sides of a conflict: the winner and loser, although it will be a lopsided battle for one of the two parties. Because of this dual nature some tarot scholars have found it difficult to assign a definite meaning to the card, but the opposing meanings are easily reconciled.

TEN OF STAKES

'Killed by many spears, and thus he died.'

In late 1476 the Ottoman governors from the border region of Wallachia led an invasion to remove him once and for all. Vlad Dracula found himself under heavy attack from Turkish troops and boyars supporting his rival, Basarab III, and was killed on the field either after being mistaken for a member of the enemy army or being attacked from behind by a soldier who had been bribed into slitting his throat. Of the 200 Moldavian troops protecting him only 10 escaped with their lives. When Vlad met his death he did not go down without a fight; he fought off at least 10 men, killing five of them, before succumbing to his wounds.

Divinatory meaning: pain, difficulties, oppression and treachery. The Ten of Stakes can relate to an internal treachery in which your mind is not in harmony with your actions, or an overbearing but not insurmountable oppression from an external force. Unlike other cards that indicate hardship such as The Devil or The Tower, the Ten of Stakes represents events that may be overcome although with great effort. Fighting against the enemy despite overwhelming odds is a way to move forward and claim victory; giving up is never a good option.

PAGE OF STAKES

Chief falconer Hamza Bey

Hamza served Murad II as an able military governor, and was appointed commander of the Ottoman navy by Mehmed II during the siege of Constantinople. Following the fall of the Byzantine Empire he was tasked with mopping up resistance throughout the Greek Isles, a mission that met with mixed results before being halted by the virtually impregnable defences of the Knights Hospitaller on the Isle of Rhodes.

Elevated to the rank of bey and granted governorship over the border region of Nicopolis, Hamza was responsible for monitoring the ongoing turmoil in Wallachia and remaining prepared for war if called to arms by the Ottoman sultan. He was also appointed chief falconer in the Ottoman imperial court, a prestigious office that afforded the holder direct access to the sultan.

In 1460 Hamza was selected by the sultan to lead a security delegation to Wallachia while Vlad Dracula was brought to the sultan's court for negotiations, and was present during the initial meeting between Vlad and the Ottoman diplomat Thomas Katabolinos. Vlad felt Hamza's presence was a prelude to an attack and led an attack of his own, surprising the envoy and slaughtering nearly everyone present.

Divinatory meaning: a faithful servant, an envoy or a lover. The Page of Stakes is a man in search of something; he has a message to deliver and may be a stranger in a strange land, although he is a dear friend and envoy on behalf of another. It may represent a person who is extremely close such as a brother, co-worker or classmate. They will be helpful and possibly bring good news, or at least solid advice in the future. The correlation between a falconer and the Page of Stakes is especially strong because pages represent the airy side of any element – in this case the element of fire.

KNIGHT OF STAKES

Voivode Basarab III

Basarab III's two brothers were both executed by Vlad Dracula, so his desire to sit upon the throne was as much motivated by revenge as it was by gaining personal power. Basarab shifted his alliance to whichever faction supported his attempts to regain the throne, entering into an alliance with Hungary's King Matthias and Moldavia's Prince Stephen III when Radu launched an invasion of Transylvania in 1475. Radu's men were slaughtered, with many historians believing Basarab personally killed Radu.

In 1476 Mehmed II ordered an invasion of Transylvania, Moldavia and Wallachia and Basarab paid homage to him, a betrayal against his Christian allies that proved to be his undoing. Stephen and Matthias unleashed Vlad Dracula from captivity and allowed him free rein but Vlad was killed in battle against Basarab's troops. Basarab was killed during the Battle of Breadfield while fighting against his nephew and former Ottoman masters.

Divinatory meaning: departure, absence, a change of residence and taking initiative. The Knight of Stakes is viewed as a negative character due to his shifting loyalties. The knight has an affinity with mercury, which can represent a desire for exploration and travel although not for pleasure. The Knight of Stakes has a strong connection to family matters and, more specifically, family quarrels based on a common event in the family's history. On the positive side the Knight of Stakes does have a yearning for knowledge and a desire to search out the unknown.

QUEEN OF STAKES

Lady Kalinikia, Vlad's great-grandmother

The wife of Radu I, Lady Kalinikia was generous and pious, having retreated to an Orthodox monastery following the death of her husband in 1383 until her own death at a very old age in 1439. She was either the daughter of a Serbian ruler or a Byzantine princess, the latter theory arising because she was of the Orthodox faith and her name is a variation of the name of a Byzantine fortress, Kaliakra.

However, 'Kalinikia' was not even her actual birth name. She was born with the first name Ana, most likely to a noble boyar family in western Wallachia. Murals of her in two different monasteries identify her as both 'Ana' and 'Kalinikia', which has led some scholars to propose that Radu I had two wives. However, the name 'Kalinikia' was commonly used by women when they joined an Orthodox monastery.

Divinatory meaning: fondness, attraction, command and intuition. The Queen of Stakes is an honourable woman inclined to provide help and encouragement. She is good natured and able to follow her intuition, which may indicate that gut feelings should always be followed. There is a slight connection with money, growth and physical things, perhaps suggesting the queen has a love of material gifts.

KING OF STAKES

Emperor Sigismund

Sigismund of Luxembourg had a tremendous amount of influence over mediaeval Europe during his 50-year reign as king of Hungary. He organised numerous crusades against the Ottoman Empire, culminating in the disastrous Battle of Nicopolis on the Danube River. In 1408 Sigismund founded the Order of the Dragon, an order of chivalry with the express goal of repelling attacks from the Ottoman Empire and regaining some of Christianity's lost prestige from the early crusades. Vlad Dracul was invested as a knight in the order in 1431.

Sigismund's ability as a political leader surpassed his military conquests; he successfully expanded the borders of Hungary by negotiating to take the crowns from weaker monarchs. This complex network of political intrigues and interpersonal relationships helped him ascend to the dignity of Holy Roman emperor in 1433, just four years before his death at the age of 69.

Divinatory meaning: a passionate and honest leader, nobility and action. The King of Stakes is both a dark and good character with severe qualities that are nevertheless noble; his symbol is the royal lion. This card indicates intelligence and honesty in a person, along with inherent authority. As the chief embodiment of the Suit of Wands, there is an intimation of fiery passion and a tendency to take action when necessary.

ACE OF SWORDS

The Ottoman kilij

Historians are not certain what kind of sword Vlad Dracula may have used; it could have been anything from a Spanish broadsword to a Japanese katana. The voivode of Wallachia would have been invested with a gold crown, the national flag, the sceptre of office and a sword, sabre and lance. The sabre was most likely the curved style of sword known as a *kilij*, in the mid-1400s a relatively new invention created in the workshops of Ottoman swordsmiths by adapting the existing designs of Turko-Mongol cavalry swords. Its design allowed for maximum stabbing power, making it a formidable weapon in the hands of a trained warrior.

Among the items Vlad inherited from his father was an exquisite broadsword made of Toledo steel, which might have been too precious to risk being damaged in battle. Although it may never be known for certain what style of sword or sabre Vlad used, we can assume he used several different types throughout his lifetime. In mediaeval Europe the quality and quantity of an army's swords were a mark of their capability on the battlefield.

Divinatory meaning: triumph, conquest, valiant action, thinking, conflict, great force in both love and hatred. The Ace of Swords indicates a strong outpouring of force; it may be love, anger or simply your own energy in the beginning of some new adventure. There is great courage in this card and the sword should eliminate any sense of doubt, leaving only confidence in your actions. The concept of beginnings and success in trials overcome is very much present.

Although his favourite weapon was the impaling stake, Vlad Dracula ruled by the sword. His nation was perpetually at war, and just as guns are today the machinery of battle, in mediaeval Europe the quality and quantity of an army's swords were a mark of their capability on the battlefield.

TWO OF SWORDS

Cutting the ears off a Turkish slave

The warfare of mediaeval Europe was far more ghastly and brutal than is the warfare of today. Although artillery was beginning to prove useful in the 1400s, it was not widespread and soldiers were expected to get their hands dirty if they hoped to survive against the enemy. Many chroniclers relate details concerning Vlad's hands-on approach to violence and particularly the cutting of lips, noses and ears. When Vlad led a strike against the Ottoman city of Nicopolis he hacked the ears, noses and heads off men, women and children, gathered them in a bag and sent them to Hungary as proof of his success.

From the Byzantine era the removal of victims' ears and noses was a common practice among soldiers as evidence of victory, and soldiers were paid an extra bonus based on the number of victims they had killed. It was much easier to transport small parts of the head to prove their ability as a warrior rather than the entire head. During his sojourn in the Middle East, Napoleon commented that Ottoman soldiers seemed more interested in removing ears from the dead than they did in actually fighting against the French.

Divinatory meaning: indecision, trouble and inner balance. As a card of balance and decision the Two of Swords can be very confusing, as it combines the meaning of the twos of other suits.

The inability to make a decision between two courses of action will inevitably lead to trouble as you seek inner balance.

In the image a Turkish slave kneeling to accept his fate has already lost one ear and is about to lose a second. Vlad's force represents the unknown future you cannot properly see and against which you are powerless. However, there is hope because the slave is going to live but only after balance has been achieved by the removal of his second ear.

The nailing of the turbans

THREE OF SWORDS

The nailing of the Turbans

Vlad received a delegation of diplomats from Mehmed II at his Târgovişte court. The diplomats bowed in greeting but failed to remove their turbans, which Vlad felt was disrespectful. He asked the envoys why they had not removed their turbans and they replied: 'Sir, it is our custom not to remove our headgear. Our ruler follows the same practice.'

Vlad signalled his guards to seize the entire delegation and told them: 'If that is your custom, let me strengthen it for you.' He had long nails driven through their turbans into their skulls then sent the envoys back to the sultan, telling them that future delegations would receive the same treatment if they failed to pay him the respect due a sovereign monarch.

Divinatory meaning: sorrow, absence, worry, bad news and internal difficulties. The troubles indicated by the Three of Swords are primarily internal or mental. They may be the result of overthinking, of having too many options or the difficulties inherent in making a final decision. It is a card of bad news, more specifically bad news in the case of a relationship. Although the traditional imagery of the card shows three swords through a heart it does not necessarily indicate the end of a relationship, but it could mean prolonged separation or distance between two people that may cause a strain.

FOUR OF SWORDS

Tomb of Vlad Dracula

Vlad Dracula's death occurred in the marshy woods north of Bucharest. Snagov Monastery is the most likely location for his tomb because the original chronicles indicate Snagov's monks retrieved his body from the battlefield out of loyalty to their old master and buried it inside the sanctuary.

In 1933 an archaeology team found a burial vault that contained the remains of a male skeleton draped in fine clothing with a gold crown and other jewellery placed beside the body. It was obviously the body of a voivode and was thought to be Vlad's body. The tomb of Vlad Dracula exists as a shrine to his life as one of the great voivodes of Romanian history. A gold-plated portrait of Vlad adorns the tomb and candles are lit in his memory.

Divinatory meaning: rest, reprieve and temporary retreat or exile. The Four of Swords is the calm before the storm, a momentary step away from the chaos of daily life. The rest component can be connected with the eternal rest that accompanies death. There is a sense of stillness connected with this card and the meditative state of a calm mind. Although it indicates exile or retreat this is not necessarily negative, as the exile would be one that is self-imposed such as that of a hermit or monk who is seeking closeness with divine energies.

FIVE OF SWORDS

Radu attacking Poenari Castle

After Mehmed II failed to defeat Vlad Dracula he turned back to the Ottoman Empire, leaving Radu the Handsome in charge of eliminating his own brother. Radu stormed the countryside, rallying the boyars to his cause by reminding them of Vlad's cruel acts and heavy taxes. Radu knew he could hold the title of voivode if Vlad were out of the picture.

Radu knew exactly where his brother would be hiding: Poenari Castle. He positioned the janissary corps in a ring around the base of the mountain then hauled Turkish artillery pieces to a clearing in the hills across the valley. The siege was ineffective as the sultan had given Radu light bombards only and Poenari's walls were too thick to breech. The castle could only be taken by force so Radu's men scrambled up the mountain trail, but their prize had slipped away in the night. Even though his main objective was thwarted, Radu had finally gained the upper hand in the conflict for Wallachia's throne. His brother's last stronghold had been overtaken and Vlad was now a fugitive.

Divinatory meaning: empty victory, defeat, dishonour and destruction. The Five of Swords represents a feeling of being wronged by the world and the bitterness that follows, along with the negative emotions that can cause you to sabotage yourself and be your own worst enemy. It can indicate a fear of success and of accepting responsibility when confidence is lacking. It is not a card of total defeat, but rather represents a low point in the struggle that can be redeemed.

Radu's assault on Poenari Castle began as an even playing field: he had guns and soldiers, while Vlad held the high ground in an impregnable fortress. If it were not for the unfortunate suicide of his wife weakening his morale and his decision to flee in the night, Vlad would have fought a ferocious battle to repel the invaders and hold the fortress. However, knowing that the boyars of Wallachia were against him and all was essentially lost, Vlad gave up his castle and fled to preserve his own life.

SIX OF SWORDS

Wallachians crossing the frozen Danube

In February 1462 Vlad Dracula realised the Ottoman sultan would never stop regarding Wallachia as a vassal state and that if he failed to prevent Turkish dominance Mehmed II would begin sending soldiers rather than envoys to demand tribute. Vlad crossed the frozen Danube River with a fighting force under the cover of night. The Wallachian army tore up and down the border, attacking every settlement and fortress and sparing no one. Civilians and soldiers were hacked to pieces and impaled on stakes.

More than 23,000 native Bulgarians and Ottoman soldiers were brutally murdered in the savage attacks: Christian or Muslim, man or woman, old or young. Vlad noted his numbers did not include 'those burned alive in their houses, or whose heads were not presented to our officers'.

Divinatory meaning: a journey by water or a route or road. This card has much to do with travel and movement, the traditional imagery showing a ferryman pushing his passengers across a calm body of water toward a distant shore. Also indicated is a pathway to somewhere a person has not travelled before, for instance a spiritual quest and the rewards that lie beyond. There may be a connection with sadness or sorrow but this is not absolute.

SEVEN OF SWORDS

Vlad's narrow escape

In one of Vlad Dracula's most challenging moments his brother Radu the Handsome held him under siege at Poenari Castle. After being forewarned by Radu's Wallachian soldiers loyal to Vlad that they intended to assault the castle in the morning, Vlad's wife threw herself off the tower walls into the river below. This act shook his morale and spurred his decision to vacate the fortress during the night.

Vlad and a small contingent of soldiers escaped through a secret tunnel and descended from the mountain. They put their horses' shoes on backwards to confuse the enemy and enlisted the aid of the seven Dobrin brothers, members of a local peasant clan. Despite his best efforts, Vlad was eventually captured and taken to prison.

Divinatory meaning: attempted plan that may fail and hopes and wishes. The Seven of Swords suggests a plan that may lead to disaster but could be successful. The plan has an element of trickery or something evil contained in it, so it could be best for everyone if it doesn't succeed. There is a strong connection with hopes and dreams, although they will require significant work for them to materialise. The effort might be minimised by taking a short cut to get the job done more quickly.

EIGHT OF SWORDS

Vlad led to Hungarian captivity

Just a few weeks after Vlad's narrow escape from Poenari Castle King Matthias recognised Radu the Handsome as Wallachia's rightful ruler. Vlad was captured by the Czech mercenary commander Jan Jiskra at Königstein fortress and turned over to the king. Matthias was surprised to discover news of Vlad's capture was eliciting significant consternation from his allies, so he presented documents proving Vlad was preparing to betray Hungary. As his removal from power would bring stability to the region his imprisonment was accepted as a necessary evil. When he was finally released, much of Vlad's brashness had faded and he was killed in battle shortly after.

Unfortunately, Radu began a campaign against Transylvania and Moldavia on behalf of his ally that resulted in a period of extreme instability throughout Wallachia, until the country became an Ottoman vassal state under Vlad the Monk in 1482.

Divinatory meaning: bad news, crisis, indecision, and a condition of servitude. The Eight of Swords indicates something bad is coming or has already occurred. A condition of bondage or of an inability to act will result, but this will be a temporary condition. It may seem as though there is finality in this card but there is not, because it simply represents a circumstance in which a person needs patience to wait to be able to proceed as they wish.

The traditional image of the Eight of Swords shows a woman standing among a field of swords bound and blindfolded, leading some scholars to connect the card with emotional or relationship troubles caused by a woman or health issues arising from relations with a promiscuous partner.

NINE OF SWORDS

Radu the Handsome and Sultan Mehmed

Radu the Handsome and Mehmed II's relationship began after 1444, when Vlad Dracul left the court of Mehmed's father, Murad II, and his sons were left in Murad's care to ensure their father's loyalty. After Vlad's death in 1447 Radu remained in the court of the sultan, who was preparing to abdicate in favour of his son, Mehmed.

Mehmed had noticed Radu's beautiful features and made a sexual overture towards the 13-year-old boy. The overwhelmed Radu stabbed his attacker in the thigh then fled. After Mehmed promised him that no harm would befall him, the two young men became constant companions and eventually consensual lovers. Their relationship proved to be of great benefit to Radu, who in 1462 was given command of the janissary corps and became voivode of Wallachia with Mehmed's support after a difficult campaign to oust his brother from the throne.

Divinatory meaning: despair, cruelty, intolerance and a bad omen. The Nine of Swords is a card of absolute misery and sadness. It is not necessarily a card of death or endings, but more of sorrow and despair. The essence of the Nine of Swords is intolerance, especially religious intolerance, and hard immovable opinions. Traditional imagery depicts a woman crying in her bed, in mental anguish or emotional despair rather than physical danger.

TEN OF SWORDS

Michael Szilágyi sawn in half

The unfortunate fate of the former regent of Hungary, Count Michael Szilágyi, set in motion the events of 1462 that ultimately led to Vlad Dracula's downfall. Mehmed II had just conquered the few remaining Serbian outposts governed by Szilágyi, who was captured by Ottoman commander Mihaloğlu Ali Bey. Bey took his prisoner to Constantinople to appear before Mehmed to decide his ultimate fate. As punishment for refusing to divulge the military capabilities of the Hungarian army, Mehmed ordered that Szilágyi be hung upside down and slowly sawn in half. Astoundingly, Szilágyi held his tongue and revealed nothing during the procedure.

The death of Michael Szilágyi enraged King Matthias and Vlad Dracula, both of whom considered him a mentor and friend. Vlad assaulted Turkish envoys by nailing their turbans to their heads and sent them back to Mehmed as a warning. Some of the cruelty he displayed during his 1462 campaign against the Ottomans may be attributed to his desire for revenge for the manner in which Szilágyi was executed.

Divinatory meaning: pain, affliction, sadness, despair and complete and total ruin. The unpleasant Ten of Swords is an indicator of heaviness of the soul and of the poor material conditions a person may face. The ending proposed by this card does not signal a rebirth like the Death card but the ending of an enterprise, relationship or journey that will cause pain, misery and hardship. Traditional imagery shows a body stabbed through with swords against a dark sky, but the suggestion of a mortal death is not so relevant here as is a death of the soul.

PAGE OF SWORDS

Michael Szilágyi, regent of Hungary

Michael Szilágyi's relationship with his nephew was extremely tense owing to Matthias' desire to rule without assistance from a regent. The young king had little regard for Szilágyi's position, but when several military commanders and nobles began to turn against him Matthias enlisted his uncle's help. After resigning as regent of Hungary, Szilágyi was stationed as a military commander along the border between Serbia, Romania and the Ottoman Empire. He defended the Futak fortress against a Turkish incursion but was captured in 1460 by the same general he had defeated, taken to Constantinople and sawn in half.

It's possible Szilágyi contributed to Vlad's military training, with Vlad once referring to him as his 'master and brother'. When Vlad was released from Hungarian captivity in 1475 he was invited to marry Michael's daughter, Justina Szilágyi, a marriage that strengthened his political ties with Matthias.

Divinatory meaning: authority, overseeing of activities and a spy or diplomat. The Page of Swords possesses great skill in communication and knowledge, which may be clandestine as in the form of information gained through espionage. Being a page it is the most airy card in the airy Suit of Swords, therefore this person will have heavy influence from the realm of Gemini.

KNIGHT OF SWORDS

Captain-General John Hunyadi

John Hunyadi was appointed voivode of Transylvania in 1441, which placed him in direct conflict with Vlad Dracul. In 1443 Hunyadi was made commander-in-chief of the Hungarian crusade to expel the Turkish army from Serbia and Bulgaria. Also joining the fight were Count Michael Szilágyi and Vlad Dracul, who had mustered his troops to support the crusade and redeem himself for his former support of the Ottomans. In 1446 Hunyadi was appointed governor of Hungary; he added property and castles to his personal estate and attacked any regional ruler who defied his rule. He invaded Wallachia and placed Vladislav II on the throne, usurping Vlad Dracul and commanding he be executed.

Hunyadi mounted another crusade against the Ottoman army in Serbia and Bulgaria, in which he succeeded. While celebrating his newfound success he contracted the plague and died after a brief illness. His heroic deeds were never forgotten, and two years after his death his son Matthias Corvinus was elected king of Hungary.

Divinatory meaning: bravery, heroic action, war, wrath, strife and opposition. The Knight of Swords represents a military man or a police officer, someone who fights on behalf of an authority figure. It will be a person who bears weapons with the capability of righting the wrongs previously committed by an enemy. In the context of war and conflict, this card represents painful memories and suffering from the past that perhaps cannot be changed but can be avenged in the present.

John Hunyadi may well have been the original inspiration for the Knight of Wands, a card described by traditional occultists as an 'armed man under the rule of the emperor'. This description fit Hunyadi like a tailored suit of armour: in his position as a soldier and military governor, Hunyadi consistently attempted to seek revenge against the Ottoman Empire and to undo their territorial conquests by means of his own personal crusade on behalf of the entire country.

QUEEN OF SWORDS

Queen Mother Elizabeth Szilágyi

Elizabeth Szilágyi was an influential and important figure in Hungarian politics, especially during the chaotic period following the death of Emperor Sigismund to the coronation of her own son Matthias as king. As the wife of John Hunyadi and a noblewoman in her own right, Elizabeth held tremendous sway in Hungary while her husband was abroad fighting battles or governing his territories in Transylvania and Serbia.

Hunyadi's death created a dangerous situation for Elizabeth and her children. In 1457 her oldest son, Ladislaus, murdered Count Ulrich II after the count accused him of failing to pay his father's debts. He was arrested and promptly beheaded. Elizabeth and her brother Michael Szilágyi fomented a civil insurrection against the king, who fled to Vienna where he fell ill and died. Two months later Matthias was proclaimed king of Hungary and Elizabeth was declared Queen Mother. In her later life she retired from the political sphere and became a patron of Catholic monasteries and churches throughout the Hungarian territories.

Divinatory meaning: a skilful, brave, clever woman, mourning, sadness and all forms of artistic expression. The Queen of Swords is a woman who rules by utilising her natural physical gifts. She is familiar with sorrow, as she has experienced loss throughout her life. This card may also represent a woman who has been separated from a male figure through divorce or widowhood. The Queen of Swords is also connected to art and artistic expression of all kinds, especially wealth derived from challenging artistic work.

Elizabeth Szilágyi's existence as the wife of the great and influential Captain-General John Hunyadi was only the prelude to her second act as mother of a great and noble king. She was directly responsible for this transition, but was only spurred to it after the murder of her eldest son. Had she not experienced this tragic heartbreak, coming so closely after the death of her husband, the world might never have noted her name.

KING OF SWORDS

King Matthias of Hungary

King Matthias of Hungary assumed the throne at the age of 14 after the death of King Ladislaus V. Although young he was ready to meet the challenges of ruling the nation, and to the surprise of many was a skilled ruler. During Vlad's longest reign as Wallachian voivode from 1456 to 1462 and due to his shifting loyalties, Matthias was alternatively an ally or an enemy. In 1462 Vlad attempted to make good on his lacklustre loyalty by waging a full-scale war against Mehmed II but it wasn't enough to satisfy Matthias, who had Vlad captured and imprisoned in Hungary. When their relationship eventually warmed, Vlad served as an adviser and confidant to the king.

Matthias found disappointment in three brides, none of whom bore him living children.

Divinatory meaning: power and command, a friend and counsellor, judgement, law and authority. The King of Swords fights battles and wins wars, although this does not necessarily make him warlike or overly aggressive. This is a tactician who can make a plan and put it into successful action and whose rule is not questioned. This card denotes the royal spirit even more than the kings of other suits. The King of Swords can also be a friend or adviser who provides guidance about the future and may be helpful even when the problem at hand is not an actual conflict.

BIBLIOGRAPHY

Anonymous, *Die Geschicht Dracole Waide*, Nuremberg, 1488.

Bogdan, Ioan. *Documente Privitoare La relaţiile Ţării Româneşti Cu Braşovul şi Cu Ţara Ungureascâ: în Sec. XV şi XVI*. Institutul De Arte Grafice 'Carol Göbl' S-r I. St. Rasidescu, 1905.

Bogdan, Ioan. *Vlad Tepes si Naratiunile Germane si Rusesti Asupra Lui*. Editura Librariei Socecu & Comp, 1896.

Cazacu, Matei and Marie Nizet. *Dracula*. Brill, 2017.

DaLezze, Donado and Ion Ursu. *Historia Turchesca (1300–1514)*. Ed. Acad. Române, 1910.

Dan, Peter. 'Psycho-biographical considerations about Vlad the Impaler also known as Dracula'. https://www.researchgate.net/publication/271386571_Psycho-biographical_considerations_about_Vlad_theImpaler_also_knons_as_Dracula, December 2014.

Diaconovici, Corneliu. *Enciclopedia română*. Editura şi Tiparul Lui W. Krafft, 1898.

Dickens, David B. and Elizabeth Miller. 'Michael Beheim, German Meistergesang, and Dracula'. Papers from the International Conference of the Fantastic in the Arts, 2003.

Efrosin, *The Tale of Prince Dracula*. Translated by Jan Howlett. Jesus College, Cambridge.

Encausse, Gérard. *The Tarot of the Bohemians: The most ancient book in the world.* Translated by A.P. Morton, 1892.

Florescu, Radu R. and Raymond T. McNally. *Dracula, Prince of Many Faces: His life and his times*. Little Brown & Company, 2009.

Florescu, Radu R. and Raymond T. McNally. *In Search of Dracula: The history of Dracula and vampires*. Robson Books, 1977.

Gilgore, Daniel. 'The Establishment of the First Metropolitan See of Wallachia'. Proceedings of Harvard Square Symposium: The Future of Knowledge, vol. 1, pp. 146–60, April 2016.

Hasan, Mihai Florin (2013). 'Aspecte ale relaţiilor matrimoniale munteano-maghiare din secolele XIV-XV'. Revista Bistriţei. XXVII: 128–59.

'Listă De Mitropoliți Ai Ungrovlahiei'. Wikipedia, Wikimedia Foundation, 10 June 2019, https://ro.wikipedia.org/wiki/List%C4%83_de_mitropoli%C8%9Bi_ai_Ungrovlahiei.

Liviu Cîmpeanu. 'Basarab Laiotă, domn al Ţării Româneşti: preliminarii la o monografie'. Studii şi Materiale de Istorie Medie (SMIM) XXXII: 145–72.

Liviu Cîmpeanu. 'Basarab Laiotă, Ştefan cel Mare şi Matia Corvinul la 1477'. Analele Putnei 2: 7–16.

McDonald, William C. *'Whose Bread I Eat': The Song-Poetry of Michel Beheim*. Kümmerle, 1981.

Michałowicz, Konstanty and Benjamin A. Stolz. *Memoirs of a Janissary/Konstantin Mihailović*. Published under the Auspices of the Joint Committee on Eastern Europe, American Council of Learned Societies, by the Department of Slavic Languages and Literatures, University of Michigan, 1975.

Ouspensky, P.D. *The Symbolism of the Tarot*. Translated by A.L. Pogossky. Trood Printing and Publishing Company, St Petersburg, Russia, 1913.

Panaitescu, Petre P. and Lazăr Gheorghe. *Mircea Cel Bătrân*. Corint, 2000.

Petcu, Marcu-Marian et al. *Pagini Din Istoria Monahismului Ortodox în Revistele Teologice Din România*. Editura Bibliotecii Naţionale a României, 2011.

Scarlat, Filip-Lucian. 'L'uniatisme en Moldavie et le Role Des Jesuites Apres le Concile de Florence et Jusqu'à la Fin Du Xvii Siecle'. https://www.academia.edu/1077188/LUNIATISME_EN_MOLDAVIE_ET_LE_ROLE_DES_JESUITES_APRES_LE_CONCILE_DE_FLORENCE_ET_JUSQU%C3%80_LA_FIN_DU_XVII_SIECLE.

Ştefulescu, Alexandru. *Documente Slavo-române Relative La Gorj, 1406-1665*. N.D. Miloşescu, 1908.

Thierens, A.E. and Arthur Edward Waite. *The General Book of the Tarot: Containing the Astrological Key to the Tarot-System Published for the First Time*. W. Rider, 1928.

Wey, William et al. *The Itineraries of William Wey: Fellow of Eton College to Jerusalem, A.D. 1458 and A.D. 1462; and to Saint James of Compostella, A.D. 1456*. J.B. Nichols, 1857.

Zamfirache, Cosmin Pătraşcu. 'Adolescenta Care i-a Sucit Minţile Lui Ştefan Cel Mare. Ascensiunea Misterioasă a Unei Copile De 16 Ani De La Prizonieră La Doamnă a Moldovei.' *Adevarul.ro*, 7 August 2015.

Waite, Arthur Edward and Pamela Coleman Smith. *The Pictorial Key to the Tarot: Being fragments of a secret tradition under the veil of divination*. W. Rider, 1911.

ABOUT THE AUTHOR

Travis McHenry is widely regarded as being one of the foremost occultists of the modern era. He has lectured and written about the history of the tarot and is the author of *Occult Tarot* and *Angel Tarot*. He is a native of rural Pennsylvania and grew up surrounded by the folklore of the Appalachian Mountains.

As a teenager Travis was obsessed with vampires and even tried to convince a local carpenter to build a coffin for him to sleep in. After he read a biographical account of the real Prince Dracula, Travis became increasingly fascinated by the actuality behind the myth of Stoker's vampire. This obsession eventually led him on a journey through the wild countryside of Romania to the sites where Vlad Dracula earned his infamous reputation. He left no stone unturned on this expedition, descending into the only crypt in Transylvania and exploring the hillside where Vlad was reputed to have dipped his bread in the blood of his victims.

www.bloodstone.info

ACKNOWLEDGEMENTS

I would like to gratefully acknowledge the following.

Antoaneta Granberg, associate professor of Slavic languages at Gothenburg University, for her generous assistance translating the Old Church Slavonic on the tombstones at Dealu Monastery.

Andrew A. for his confirmations and corrections of my Latin.

The people of Romania, who were very kind and inviting while I was touring their country; especially the friendly street kids of Sighișoara and the proprietor of Pensiunea La Cetate, who made my stay at Poenari Castle an experience to remember.

Authors Radu R. Florescu and Raymond T. McNally for the heavy research upon which the foundation of this book (and every other book about Vlad the Impaler) has been built.

I owe a huge debt to Bram Stoker for using his wit and imagination to transform an obscure 15th-century Balkan prince into a legendary character of literature, film, television and theatre.

ALSO BY TRAVIS

ANGEL TAROT – *ISBN 9781925924206*

Go beyond the traditional angel tarot decks with this set of 72 angels of the Kabbalah (or Shem HaMephorash) cards.

Since the beginning of time, we have been drawn to the magnificence and grandeur of angels. Now using original sigils, summoning seals and pentacles from ancient grimoires, the choirs of angelic hierarchy from the kabbalah are shared with their divine names to invoke the true energies of these sacred, majestic beings into your life.

OCCULT TAROT – *ISBN 9781925924213*

How can we possibly embrace our truest self if we never step into the dark?

Author and occultist Travis McHenry reveals the secret demons of the 17th century and conjures their powers into this unique 78 divination card set. The first tarot deck to faithfully adhere to the Solomonic principles of demon conjuration, the *Occult Tarot* draws on demons, symbols and sigils from ancient magickal grimoires, including Archidoxis Magica and the Key of Solomon.